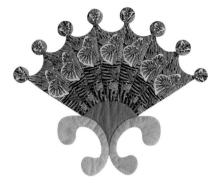

fantastic
Fans

Exquisite Quilts & Other Projects

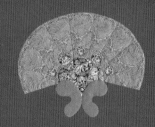

Alice Dunsdon

C&T PUBLISHING

© 2003 Alice L. Dunsdon

Editor-in-Chief: DARRA WILLIAMSON

Editor: SARAH SACKS DUNN

Copy Editor: EVA SIMONI ERB

Technical Editors: SARAH SACKS DUNN & TERESA STROIN

Proofreader: JENNI MORRISON

Cover Designer: KRISTY KONITZER

Design Director and Book Designer: ROSE SHEIFER

Illustrator: RICHARD SHEPPARD

Production Assistants: KIRSTIE L. MCCORMICK AND MATT ALLEN

Front Cover: CABBAGE ROSES, PHOTOGRAPHY BY GARRY GAY/PHOTO STYLING BY GARRY GAY AND DIANE PEDERSEN

Back Cover: FLIGHT OF FANCY SAMPLER AND PEACOCK FANS, PHOTOGRAPHY BY SHARON RISEDORPH

Photography: QUILT PHOTOGRAPHY BY SHARON RISEDORPH. PHOTO ON PAGE 3 BY GARRY GAY/PHOTO STYLING BY GARRY GAY AND DIANE PEDERSEN. HOW-TO PHOTOGRAPHY BY LUKE MULKS. DECORATIVE FAN PHOTOS ON PAGES 4, 5, 13, AND 17 BY CIRCE SHER. FANS ARE FROM THE COLLECTION OF PAMELA SHER AT THE HAND FAN MUSEUM OF HEALDSBURG.

Published by C&T Publishing, Inc., P.O. Box 1456, Lafayette, California, 94549

Library of Congress Cataloging-in-Publication Data

Dunsdon, Alice.
    Fantastic fans : exquisite quilts & other projects / Alice Dunsdon.
        p. cm.
    ISBN 1-57120-206-4 (trade paper)
    1. Patchwork—Patterns. 2. Quilting—Patterns. 3. Appliqué—Patterns.
    4. Fans in art. I. Title.
    TT835.D88 2003
    746.46'041—dc21
                                    2003005164

Printed in China

10 9 8 7 6 5 4 3 2 1

Contents

To my Grandson,
Grant James Dunsdon (1988—1999)
You Are Missed

Acknowledgments

We do not live through ourselves alone. Our lives are deeply intertwined with those around us—so much so that we sometimes become a product of their imaginations as much as our own. I have never found this more true than in the writing of this book: I could not have done it alone.

Profound thanks go to the staff at C&T Publishing for encouragement that kept me going when I wasn't sure I was going to make it. To Liz Aneloski for pep talks; to Diane Pedersen for her excellent photography; to Richard Sheppard for his accurate and attractive illustrations; and to Sarah Dunn for her diligence in editing; she earned her keep on this one. Thanks also to Darra Williamson, Eva Erb, Kristy Konitzer, Rose Sheifer, Kirstie McCormick, and Matt Allen.

Thanks also go to …

Joyceann Whitney who changed my thinking on color;

Granddaughter Sarah Dunsdon, who squeezed out time from her busy schedule to do my computer work;

Niece Trina Wilson and granddaughter Rebecca Brandt for the loan of their quilts for this book;

Helena Alberts, who asked my advice on fabric selections—you boosted my confidence when it was lacking;

Cindy Shaw and Jo Pierce, who found and delivered supplies to me—thanks a million;

My "You go, Girl" team: Darlene Wilson, Lois Fichter, Barb Dunsdon, Wanda Ewalt, Dorothy Whitney, Betty Lentz, Karen Krause, and Rhonda Follmer. They and many more stood firm when I wavered.

And to those who said, "You ought to write a book …"—I hope this fulfills your expectations.

Introduction
My Quilting Journey —and Yours

My first experience with quilting occurred over 20 years ago, when I quilted a Grandmother's Flower Garden top that my Mother had pieced in the 1920s. It was—and still is—a very lovely and popular pattern, but I have always been reluctant to travel a path that has been used by so many others. I discovered while doing the quilting that while I loved the process, there was something about it that made me feel boxed in.

I come by this attitude honestly—I can trace it all the way back to grade school. Every summer Mother made school clothes for my two sisters and me. She couldn't afford to buy patterns, so she would get out the mail-order catalogs and let us pick dresses from their pages. Then she would copy the dresses with determination and a treadle sewing machine. (Today this plagiarism would probably get us into some kind of trouble!)

By the time I was in high school, I was sewing some of my own clothes. We could afford patterns by then, but I wasn't happy following the instructions. It was not unusual to find me improvising—a skirt from one pattern, combined with the bodice from another. Adjust the collar slightly, change the sleeves … you get the picture. This penchant for altering the status quo eventually spilled over into other parts of my life: cooking, decorating, and landscaping.

So why not quilting? My first effort was to tamper with the traditional Grandmother's Fan pattern. My goal was to make it softer, with more curved lines, and to include appliqué. With freezer paper, a sharp pencil, and plenty of erasers on hand, I began to doodle. Out of this exercise came several fan designs, which I now present to you for your approval, in the hope that you will become inspired to forge your own path into the exciting world of creative change.

My wish is that the patterns in this book will serve as a springboard for your own adventures in quilting—I do not intend them to be "set-in-cement" patterns. By straying from the much-traveled path, you will also discover many surprises—some good, and some not so good. The good ones you will revel in; the bad, you will learn from. I think you will find that is the fun of it all.

So take my ideas—combine them, change them, tweak them—and make them your own. In so doing, enjoy what you will discover. It won't be long before you will be creating your own designs.

Happy Journey!

Fantastic TECHNIQUES

Tip

Each project has
1, 2, or 3 fans to
indicate difficulty
level. A 1-fan
project is the least
challenging; a 3-fan
project is the
most challenging.

The patterns in this book are not set in stone—they are intended for you to pick and choose from. You can make the quilts exactly as shown, or you can use elements from one or more quilts to produce your own original design. With that in mind, this chapter gives the basic techniques (and some helpful tips) for making the quilts as they are shown in the projects section. Read through these techniques, which are referred to throughout the projects, to get an idea of how I make the quilts you see. Also read through the Fantastic Fabrics chapter that follows, so you can see how I make the most of my fabrics when I plan the quilts and assemble the fans.

Fabrics

Most cotton quilting fabrics are about 40" wide after they are prewashed. Yardages given in this book are based on this measurement; you may find you have leftover fabric (never a bad thing!) after cutting the required pieces.

The yardage amounts given in the patterns assume (unless otherwise indicated, or the yardage will allow for lengthwise cuts) that any borders and sashings that are longer than 40" will be cut on the crosswise (straight) grain and pieced together.

If you prefer seamless borders and sashings, you will need to add to the yardages given and cut your strips from the lengthwise straight grain. Note that some border and sashing measurements given in the patterns are a little longer than needed—this is in case your seams aren't exactly ¼" when you sew. (You may want to cut all of your borders and sashings a little longer than specified—better to trim a little off the ends than to come up a little short!)

If you are "fussy-cutting" your fabrics (see page 14), you may need to add to the yardages given, so you can place the designs in your fabrics exactly as you want them in your fans. Tips for estimating the additional fabric needed are on page 17.

Fat quarters are recommended in some of the patterns. These are 18" x 22" cuts of fabric—instead of the traditional quarter-yard, which is only 9" wide, you get a wider piece of fabric. This is often more economical when you're working with appliqué patterns that have large pieces.

Wider fabrics (108", in some cases) are also becoming more readily available. These are very helpful when you want a seamless background or backing for your quilt. Keep an eye out for these wide fabrics when you're shopping, and recalculate your yardage requirements (you should need fewer yards of fabric when you have the extra width).

If you aren't quite sure about your yardage, here's a trick I like to use: Draw all your pattern pieces to scale on graph paper. Indicate on each piece whether it should be cut on the straight (crosswise or lengthwise) grain, or on the bias. Then, move the pieces around on another piece of graph paper, cut to represent your fabric yardage (usually 40" wide). If you take the time to make sure you purchase enough fabric up front, you can avoid that frustrating trip back to the shop for more fabric, only to discover that it's all gone.

Pressing Seams

Generally, quilters press seam allowances to one side. The rule of thumb is to press toward the darker color, so there is less "show-through" of the seam allowances. However, if this will cause bulkiness, trim away a little of the darker fabric from the seam allowance, and press the seam allowance toward the side that will make the piece the least bulky. I give pressing recommendations in the patterns where it makes a difference; otherwise, use your best judgment.

When you press diagonal seams (such as when you piece borders or sashings) or bias strips (for bindings or Celtic strips), press them open for less bulk.

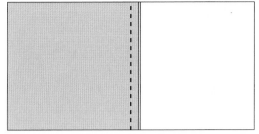

Trim dark fabric to prevent show-through.

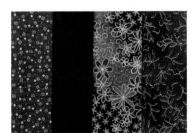

Press diagonal seams open.

🐚 Tip

The seamline in a pieced border or sashing is less noticeable when you sew it together with a diagonal seam.

Color Selection

Color can be a fearsome thing—or it can be a delight. Don't let color intimidate you before you start! Just keep a few simple concepts in mind, and you'll never—well, rarely—fail.

Color is the element that adds depth to your quilt, which is really just a flat canvas. Color is divided into values, which describe the lightness or darkness of a color. When you are selecting colors for a quilt, you will generally want to include light, medium, and dark values of fabrics.

Light colors—and colors that are "grayed" or muted—tend to recede into the background; therefore light colors are good choices for the backgrounds of your quilts. These fabrics generally don't call attention to themselves.

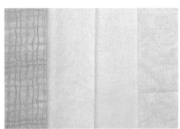

Light fabrics

Dark and bright fabrics

Medium fabrics

Dark and pure, bright colors jump out at the viewer. In the patterns in this book, the motifs—the fans, butterflies, and flowers—are the focus, so use dark and/or bright, interesting fabrics to make them come forward and call attention to themselves.

Medium colors—the colors between the lights and darks—are best used in supporting roles. Choose mediums for sashings, borders, and other elements that support the main motifs.

In painting, you mix your own colors until you get just the right light, medium, or dark color you want. With fabrics, the colors are already mixed—all you need to do is go shopping to find just the right ones.

Drawing Circles

Some of the patterns in this book use a circle to frame the focal point. This gives the appearance of a picture that has been matted. To draw a circle, you have several options:

- ❖ **Trace a round item.** Check your kitchen for something that's the size you want. Good candidates include a pot lid, plate, or pizza pan.
- ❖ **Use a compass.** A drafting compass can be set to draw accurate circles up to about 12" across.
- ❖ **Get out the string.** For larger circles, you'll need a straight pin and a piece of string that's at least half as long as your circle will be across. Fold a piece of freezer paper into quarters, and push the pin into the folded corner.

Tie the string to the pin, then tie a pencil to the other end. You can draw as large or small a circle as you want. Cut along your drawn line through all four layers, and you'll have your circle template. Use it as you would any freezer paper template (see below).

 Tip

Gently press sheets of freezer paper together, shiny side to dull side, to make larger pieces for drawing bigger circles or pattern pieces.

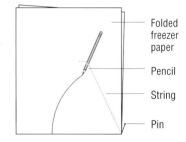

Folded freezer paper

Pencil

String

Pin

Appliqué

When I make my fan quilts, I hand appliqué the motifs to the background. I think this is the best method for the projects in this book, but you may think differently. If you want to hand appliqué, follow the directions here. Otherwise, there are many, many great books out there that can help you adapt these projects to another technique.

 Tip

Pin the layers of freezer paper together along your drawn line to hold them in place as you cut.

Freezer Paper Templates

Freezer paper templates guarantee you will get smooth curves, square corners, and accurate piecing. When working with a **symmetrical** motif (a fan or butterfly whose left and right sides are mirror images of each other), half of the motif pattern is given on the Pattern Insert.

Start with a square or rectangle of freezer paper that is the same finished size as the background you will be using. Fold the freezer paper in half lengthwise through the center.

Open the folded paper; on its dull side, trace the motif from the pattern insert, lining up your fold with the centerline of the pattern. Transfer all markings and labels onto your traced pattern, making sure to indicate "L" or "left" on each piece (you'll mark the "R" or "right" pieces when you cut out all the templates; see page 9).

Refold your freezer paper, and pin the layers together to hold them securely. Cut out the pattern around its outermost edges.

 Tip

Set aside the outer portion of your freezer paper once you have cut out the pattern; it makes a handy reference for place-ment when you are ready to appliqué the completed motif onto the background.

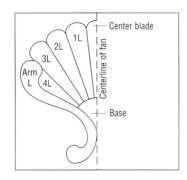

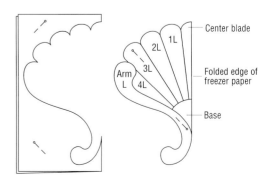

With the freezer paper still pinned and folded, cut each piece of the motif apart on the drawn lines. (Label the unlabeled "right" or "R" pieces as you cut.)

For designs that are **not symmetrical**, like some flowers and leaves, trace the entire motif onto the dull side of a piece of freezer paper, and label each piece. Then, to reverse the design so it matches the quilt as shown, pin this pattern onto another piece of freezer paper, shiny sides together. Cut out the pieces, labeling them as you go, then unpin and discard the first pattern.

Once all your freezer paper templates are completed, lay them shiny side down on the wrong side of your chosen fabrics. Place the templates at least ½" apart, to allow for ¼" seam allowances around each piece. Press the templates onto the fabric with a warm iron. Cut out each piece, making sure to cut ¼" outside the edge of the freezer paper.

Machine baste the freezer paper templates to the pieces, to prevent them from shifting or falling off as you assemble the patterns.

Assembling the Fan

The blades of most of the fans are machine stitched together. Lay out all the pieces that make up the fan wrong side up. Working from the center out, join two blades (a left and a right) to either side of the center blade.

To align the paper templates perfectly, hold the two blades up to a strong light (a bright window works well) and pin them with right sides together. Sew along the edges of the freezer paper templates, beginning at the top of the template, and continue your seam through the seam allowance at the bottom of the blade.

Open the pieces and press the seam allowances toward the center blade. Continue joining left and right blades in this manner until the fan is complete.

Preparing the Appliqué Pieces

Gather your assembled fan, fan base, and fan arms (or any other pieces you may be working with), and place them wrong side up on your ironing board. Starting on one side, turn the seam allowance over the freezer paper template, folding tightly against the edge of the template.

Where the pieces have concave (inside) curves, clip the seam allowance inside the curve to within 1/16" of the edge of the template. On convex (outside) curves, trim any tucks so the piece will lie flat.

Baste the seam allowance in place through both layers of fabric and the template. Prepare all of your appliqués in this manner. Press from the front.

Once your seam allowances are turned under and basted, you're ready to appliqué your designs to the background. Lay out your pieces on the background and pin them in place. (The outside portion of your freezer paper pattern is helpful here for placing the pieces exactly.) The pieces in each pattern are numbered so you know the sequence for sewing them to the background.

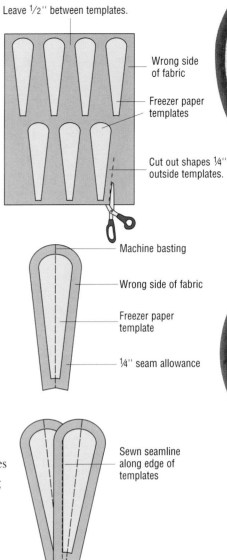

Leave ½'' between templates.

Wrong side of fabric

Freezer paper templates

Cut out shapes ¼'' outside templates.

Machine basting

Wrong side of fabric

Freezer paper template

¼'' seam allowance

Sewn seamline along edge of templates

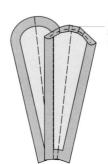

Baste through all 3 layers by hand.

Tip

Do not turn under any part of any appliqué piece that will be tucked under another piece; follow the directions indicated on the pattern.

Hand Appliqué Stitch

Tip

Any sewing thread will work for hand appliqué, but for maximum invisibility, use silk thread.

Quilters use a blind stitch to hold the designs to the background. The ultimate achievement is to make the stitch as tiny—and therefore as invisible—as possible.

To do this, choose a thread that is the same color, or a shade darker than the assembled motif.

Start your appliqué stitch on the wrong side of your background fabric. Come up through the background and the folded edge of the motif, as close to the folded edge as possible. Pull the thread through snugly. Insert the needle back down through the background fabric only, as close to the motif as possible, exactly outside where the thread came up through the motif. (This will give you the tiniest stitch.) Repeat, moving along the edge of the motif $1/16$" to $1/8$" with each stitch, until the motif is secured to the background. Knot the thread on the wrong side of the background fabric.

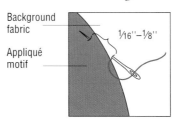

Background fabric

Appliqué motif

$1/16''$–$1/8''$

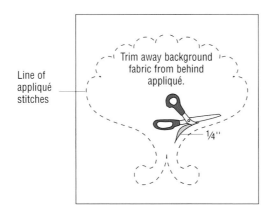

Line of appliqué stitches

Trim away background fabric from behind appliqué.

$1/4''$

Repeat the appliqué process with each piece of your motif. Follow the numbered sequence for sewing the pieces to the background, until the entire motif is complete. To reduce bulk, trim away the background behind the motif: Cut the background fabric $1/4$" inside the appliqué stitching.

Celtic Strips

Tip

Bias Bars, a pressing tool available at quilt shops, are specially designed to help press Celtic strips. They come in a set of varied widths and include complete directions.

Celtic strips are tubes of fabric that can be used for decoration on a quilt, or to cover raw edges. They are made from stretchy bias strips—strips cut diagonally across the weave of the fabric—so they easily form around curves.

The patterns specify the width to cut your bias strips. To make a Celtic strip, fold a bias strip in half lengthwise, with wrong sides together, and machine sew through both layers $1/8$" from the raw edges.

Fold the tube so that the seam is hidden beneath the two layers of fabric. With a steam iron, press both sides of the Celtic strip.

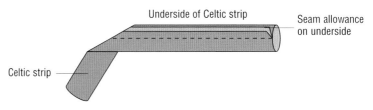

Underside of Celtic strip

Seam allowance on underside

Celtic strip

Place your Celtic strip seam side down on the background, as indicated by your pattern, and appliqué it in place by sewing both edges to the background.

Settings

Your quilt's setting is the way you arrange your blocks to show them to their best advantage. Settings can include prepared blocks, additional (alternate or spacer) blocks, supporting elements (e.g., sashings and borders), or any combination of these elements.

Straight Set

In a straight set, you place your blocks side by side, in rows and columns that are parallel to the edges of the quilt. The blocks are sewn directly to each other.

If you do not want all of the blocks to be the same, use spacer blocks that set off your prepared blocks. Try using a contrasting color, or a pieced block between the appliquéd blocks.

 Tip Use the same light fabric for both your spacer blocks and your border—the appliquéd blocks will appear to float.

Straight set with blocks side by side

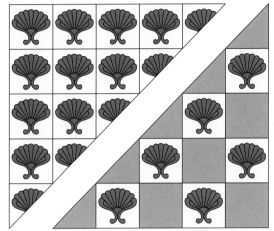

Straight set with spacer blocks

Diagonal Set

In a diagonal set, the blocks are sewn together "on point"—at a 45° angle to the sides of the quilt. The blocks can be sewn to each other, or spacer blocks can give them a little breathing room. To square out the edges of the quilt, you will need to add side triangles along the edges, as well as four corner triangles. These are usually cut oversize, then trimmed to fit later.

Diagonal set with blocks side by side

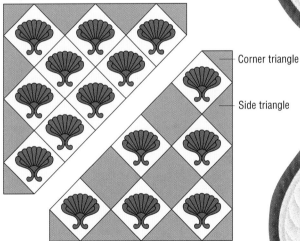

Corner triangle

Side triangle

Diagonal set with spacer blocks

Sashings

Sashings are narrow strips of fabric—often a color that contrasts with the quilt blocks—that are used to separate blocks from one another. Sashings can be used on either a straight or a diagonal set.

Where sashings intersect, some quilters like to use sashing squares, or cornerstones, as an accent. Otherwise, blocks in columns or rows have short sashing strips between them, separated by longer sashing strips.

 Tip Sashings can be extremely helpful in hiding various problems. If your blocks are slightly different sizes, or when blocks you would like next to each other have colors that clash, sashings give you a little breathing room.

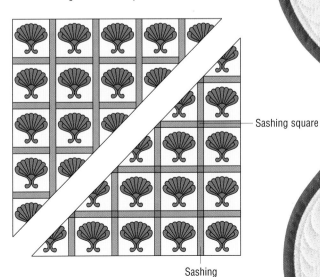

Sashing square

Sashing

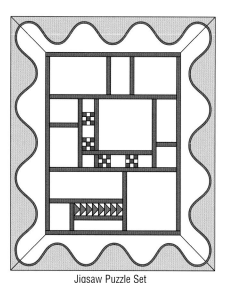

Jigsaw Puzzle Set

Jigsaw Puzzle Set

Sampler quilts are quilts that show off a collection of different quilt block designs. But what do you do when your blocks are different sizes? A jigsaw puzzle design can help. In this setting, you "fill in" the spaces left by small blocks with plain sashings, appliquéd Celtic strips, or pieced sections. The *Flight of Fancy Sampler* quilt on page 20 is a good example—several large blocks are set off by smaller strips, Nine-Patch blocks, and Flying Geese, for an overall well-balanced and interesting layout.

No-Mark Quilting

Quilting is the final touch on a quilt. But after all the work you put into making the quilt top, marking it seems tedious—and there's always the danger that the markings will be difficult to remove later. I have a handful of tricks I use when I don't want to mark my quilt top.

Geometric Backings

My favorite solution—actually, it's now an obsession of mine—is to buy geometric prints and use them as backings. My needle can follow their nice, straight lines exactly as it would a marked line—but there's no marking!

If you buy standard (40" wide) yardage, you'll need to piece your backing carefully, matching the pattern at the seams. My preference is to shop for the wider yardage that's more and more available—usually 108" wide—and buy interesting prints when I see them, for use now or later.

While the no-marking method does require you to quilt from the back of the quilt, just a little planning will help you ensure the results you want.

First, you'll need to outline the areas where you don't want to quilt, or where your pattern will change—within your motifs, certainly, and possibly in the sashings and borders. Outline quilt (or quilt in-the-ditch) around the edges of your fans and other motifs; or, baste around these areas with a contrasting color thread.

Once this is done, you're ready to quilt. Refer to the photos below for ideas; once you get the general concept, there's no end to the quilting you'll think up when a fabric strikes your fancy.

 Tip

If the print is subtle enough, use a geometric print as your background fabric, and you can use the no-mark method to quilt from the front—or even do a combination of quilting from the front and the back.

I used the herringbone pattern on this fabric two ways: I duplicated the herringbone in one section of quilting, and I used the corners as a guide for diagonal rows of stitches.

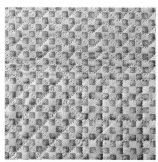

With a straight geometric print, the quilting pattern possibilities are almost endless. Here, I've quilted rows of diamonds, rows of squares, and a section of "waves."

This subtle diamond print was easy to duplicate into an elongated diamond quilting pattern. I also used it to make a staggered "bump-out" pattern of parallel lines.

Echo Quilting

If you want less of a straight-line pattern, try echo quilting to repeat the curves and shapes of the quilt motifs. Echo quilting is evenly spaced lines of quilting that surround the motif, literally "echoing" its shape. As you move farther away from the motif, the lines become less and less well defined.

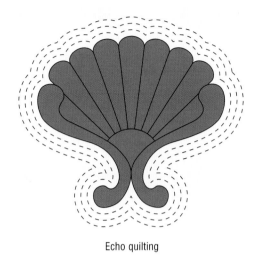

Echo quilting

Tiger Tape

Tiger Tape is a narrow roll of tape specifically designed for quilters—you can buy it at any quilt shop. The tape is marked with evenly spaced lines. When you unroll the tape and place it on your quilt, you can stitch along the edge of the tape, and your stitches will be evenly spaced.

Tiger Tape comes in different widths, so it's helpful for both straight-line quilting and echo quilting. Just place the tape along the edge of the motif, and quilt along the opposite edge of the tape. Or, cut lengths of tape and use a rotary ruler to space them evenly in any pattern you want to quilt.

Use Tiger Tape for even stitches when echo quilting.

Use Tiger Tape for even stitches when hand quilting parallel straight lines.

 Tip Lengths of Tiger Tape can be used several times. When their ability to stick to the cloth diminishes, discard them and cut new ones.

Fantastic FABRICS

Shopping for fabric can be fun—and it can be even more fun if you plan to "fussy-cut" your fabrics to highlight specific patterns, colors, or designs in the motifs you will make. Once you start, you will be surprised at how quickly you develop an eye for these special designs.

When you're out fabric shopping, always carry with you a finished-size clear plastic template of one of the blades of the fan (or of a main piece of another motif) that you are planning to make. If your fan has an odd number of blades, use the center blade; if it has an even number of blades, bring a template for one of the center blades.

To make your template, trace the finished-size pattern (don't add seam allowances!) onto the template plastic. Use the centerline that runs straight through the center of the blade on the pattern to draw a line onto the template, and use this line to help you center the blade shape on the design in the fabric.

When you place this template on fabrics as you shop, you'll be able to see right away how the pattern or design of each fabric will appear once it is part of the finished fan.

 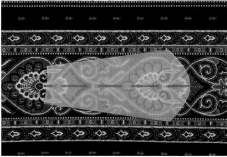

Symmetrical Designs

If you want fans that have perfect symmetry, look for fabrics that include designs that are mirror images of themselves. That is, if you draw a line down the center of a design, its two halves are identical. These fabrics will allow you to cut your fan blades on the straight grain.

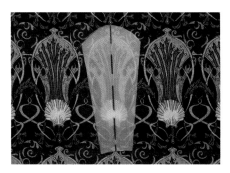 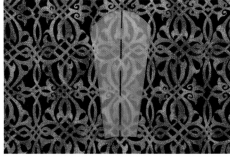

Watch for fabrics that have symmetrical designs, but the designs fall either randomly or upside down on the fabric. (These upside-downers can fool you, so be a good detective.)

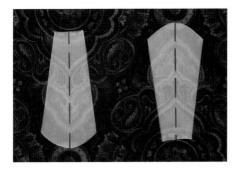

Mirror-Image Designs

If you want the right and left sides of your fan to be mirror images, be sure that you pick a fabric that has designs that are mirror images—one faces left (or up), and the other one faces right (or down).

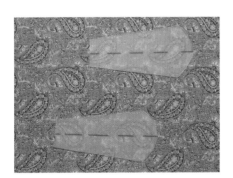

Stripes and Plaids

Stripes and plaids can be fun to work with when you're deciding on fabrics for fussy-cut designs. These straight-line patterns can be striking when the fan blades are cut on the bias, giving a chevron effect.

Plaids can be either even (the pattern is spaced the same over the entire fabric), or uneven (the pattern of lines varies in width, spacing, or both). The even plaids will give you a more uniform look. Uneven plaids can still work—they just may not match quite as well. If you fall in love with an uneven plaid, don't worry; the viewer's eye will be forgiving.

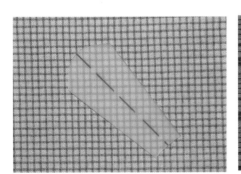

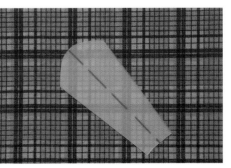

 Tip

With the template in place on the fabric, take a look for extra lines or shapes that creep in at the edges. Then, decide whether this rules out the fabric— or creates an interesting secondary design.

 Tip

Don't worry too much about the straight grain when you're cutting to highlight a specific pattern from a fabric. Your freezer-paper templates will help stabilize the cut pieces and any bias edges until your motif is completely assembled.

 Tip

If you choose a woven plaid, both sides of the fabric are usable.

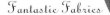

When you go looking for a stripe, don't limit your choices to traditional straight, hard-edged stripe fabrics. Remember that any fabric with a one-way design can function as a stripe. Stripes with soft edges work well, too, because matching the stripe at the seamlines doesn't have to be perfect. (Nor will it be, in most cases.)

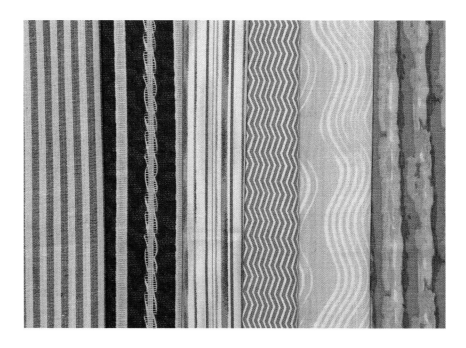

All-Over Designs

Fabrics with all-over designs can be fun to play with for fussy cutting. Move your template around from design to design—and don't forget the background. This is a terrific way to use just one piece of fabric, but get several different looks for coordinating fans in a sampler quilt.

How Much Fabric?

Fussy-cutting requires more fabric than regular cutting. To determine how much fabric you will need for fussy-cutting, first you'll need to know the number of fan blades you will be making from each pattern in the fabric—that's how many repeats of the pattern in your fabric you'll need. Count how many times the pattern appears within 9" (¼ yard), and use that number to figure out how much yardage you'll need.

But there's more: Remember that when you cut the pieces from the fabric, you'll be adding a ¼" seam allowance all the way around each piece. If there's not at least ½" between the repeats of your chosen pattern, as shown below, you may be able to use only every other repeat, and you'll have to buy twice as much fabric.

 Tip

Carry along at least two blade templates that include seam allowances when you're planning to fussy-cut. You can place these templates on the fabric to determine whether you'll need to purchase extra yardage.

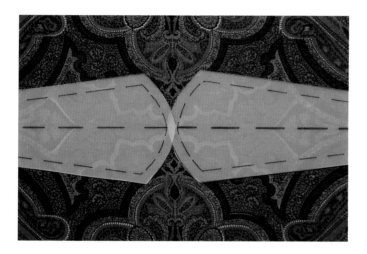

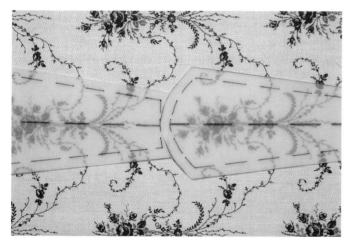

If the fussy-cutting method seems wasteful, remember that your leftover "Swiss cheese" fabric can be used again and again—other patterns in the fabric you fussy-cut might be just right for the next quilt you make!

Electric Fan Pillow

Finished size
21" x 21"

Difficulty level

This perky pillow will brighten up any space. Make a few in coordinating colors, picking and choosing from the fans and other designs on the Pattern Insert. Make your pillow bright and flamboyant or subtle and muted—whatever your taste dictates.

Materials and Cutting

FABRICS AND SUPPLIES	YARDAGE	PIECES NEEDED	NUMBER	CUT SIZE	FINISHED SIZE
Dark	Fat quarter	Fan background	1	14½" circle	14" circle
Multicolor print	1⅓ yards	Pillow front	1	21½" x 21½"	21" x 21"
		Pillow back	2	13¼" x 21½"	12¾" x 21"
Medium/bright	Fat quarter	Fan blades	9	See pattern	
Medium	4" x 5" scrap	Fan base	1	See pattern	
Light	5" x 6" scrap	Fan arms	2	See pattern	
Batting	¾ yard			25½" x 25½"	
Backing	¾ yard			25½" x 25½"	
14" pillow form				14" x 14"	

Directions

Appliqué the Fan

1. Draw a 14½" circle template onto freezer paper.

2. Cut out the template, and iron the shiny side of the freezer paper to the wrong side of the fan background fabric.

 Tip Keep the freezer paper on the fabric to prevent it from "squirming" as you cut.

3. Cut out the circle, following the edge of the template.

4. Remove the freezer paper and turn under a ¼" seam allowance around the edge of the circle. Baste, then press the seam allowance in place.

5. Appliqué the circle to the center of the pillow front. Remove the basting threads. Trim the excess pillow front fabric from behind the circle, leaving a ¼" seam allowance.

6. Use Fan 1 from the Pattern Insert, including the rounded tops of the fan blades, but not the circles that span the blades. Prepare freezer paper templates for the fan blades, base, and arms. Press the templates onto fabrics and cut out the pieces, adding seam allowances.

7. Sew the fan blades together, working from the center out, as indicated on the pattern. Press. Turn under the seam allowances. Baste. Arrange all the pieces in the center of the fan background circle, aligning the center fan blade to point straight toward (perpendicular to) one background edge.

8. Appliqué the fan pieces in place, in the order indicated on the pattern. Remove the basting threads.

9. Trim the background fabric from behind the fan, leaving a ¼" seam allowance. Remove the freezer paper templates. Press.

Quilt the Pillow Front

1. Layer and baste the backing, batting, and appliquéd pillow front.

2. Quilt as desired, through all the layers.

3. Trim the batting and backing even with the pillow front, squaring up as needed.

Assemble the Pillow

1. Hem one long side of each pillow back piece: Turn under a double fold, ¼" wide, and stitch along the double fold. Press.

2. Overlap the hemmed edges of the two pillow backs by 4", with the wrong sides facing down. Pin or baste the overlap in place (see Illustration 1).

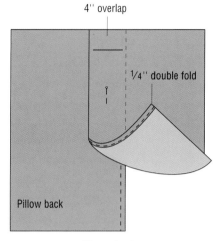

4" overlap

¼" double fold

Pillow back

Illustration 1

3. Pin the quilted pillow top to the pillow back with right sides together. Sew along the outside edge, using a ¼" seam allowance.

4. Trim the 4 corners to reduce bulk (see Illustration 2).

Trim corners

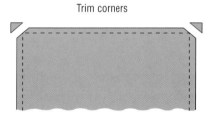

Illustration 2

5. Remove the pins or basting stitches, turn the pillow right side out through the overlap opening, and use your finger or a blunt tool to adjust the seam allowances and corners so that the pillow lies flat. Press.

6. Measure and mark 2½" inside the entire outside edge.

 Tip Freezer tape works well for marking the sewing line.

7. Sew through all layers of the pillow, following the marked line. This sewing line will form your pillow ruffle

8. Insert a 14" x 14" pillow form through the back opening.

Flight of Fancy Sampler

Finished size
50¼'' x 60¼''

Difficulty level

This quilt setting is just a jumping-off point—it has so many design possibilities, they're almost endless. You can include pieced blocks you have sitting on shelves, experiment with new color combinations, and clean out your scrap bin making this quilt. Try any and all of the designs on the Pattern Insert—just choose plain background and border fabrics to unify the quilt.

Materials and Cutting

FABRICS AND SUPPLIES	YARDAGE	PIECES NEEDED	NUMBER	CUT SIZE	FINISHED SIZE
Light	2¾ yards (for non-pieced borders)	Middle border	2	5¾'' x 62''	
			2	5¾'' x 55''	
		Block backgrounds: Section I	1	14½'' x 9½''	14'' x 9''
			1	5¼'' x 9½''	4¾'' x 9''
			1	11'' x 9½''	10½'' x 9''
		Block backgrounds: Section II	1	7½'' x 6¼''	7'' x 5¾''
			1	7½'' x 10''	7'' x 9½''
			2	3½'' x 3½''	3'' x 3''
			1	3½'' x 3¾''	3'' x 3¼''
			1	4'' x 3½''	3½'' x 3''
			1	4¼'' x 3½''	3¾'' x 3''
			1	13¾'' x 12¾''	13¼'' x 12¼''
			1	5½'' x 5½''	5'' x 5''
			1	5½'' x 10¾''	5'' x 10¼''
			16	1½'' x 1½''	1'' x 1''
		Block backgrounds: Section III	1	18½'' x 7''	18'' x 6½''
			1	5½'' x 7''	5'' x 6½''
			8*	2⅜'' x 2⅜''	
			1	12½'' x 3''	12'' x 2½''
			1	12¾'' x 14½''	12¼'' x 14''
Medium	2 yards	Outer border	2	7½'' x 56''	
			2	7½'' x 64''	
		Binding		2¼'' x 235''	
Dark (see Tip on page 23)	1¼ yards	Inner border	2	1½'' x 35''	1'' x 33¼''
			2	1½'' x 43''	1'' x 41¼''
		Sashing: Section I	2	1½'' x 9½''	1'' x 9''
		Sashing: Section II	2	1½'' x 31¾''	1'' x 31¼''
			2	1½'' x 16¾''	1'' x 16¼''
			1	1½'' x 12¾''	1'' x 12¼''
			1	1½'' x 17¾''	1'' x 17¼''
			1	1½'' x 7½''	1'' x 7''
			1	1½'' x 5½''	1'' x 5''
			1	1½'' x 3½''	1'' x 3''
		Sashing: Section III	1	1½'' x 14½''	1'' x 14''
			1	1½'' x 18½''	1'' x 18''
			1	1½'' x 12½''	1'' x 12''
			1	1½'' x 7''	1'' x 6½''
		Pieced blocks	20	1½'' x 1½''	1'' x 1''
			2**	4¼'' x 4¼''	
		Border bias		1'' x 260''	
Medium/bright and dark scraps		Appliqué shapes	See patterns		
Batting				54'' x 64''	
Backing	3⅓ yards			54'' x 64''	

*Cut each square in half diagonally to yield 16 triangles.
**Cut each square in half diagonally in both directions to yield 4 triangles (8 total triangles).

Directions

Illustration 1
Quilt Assembly Diagram

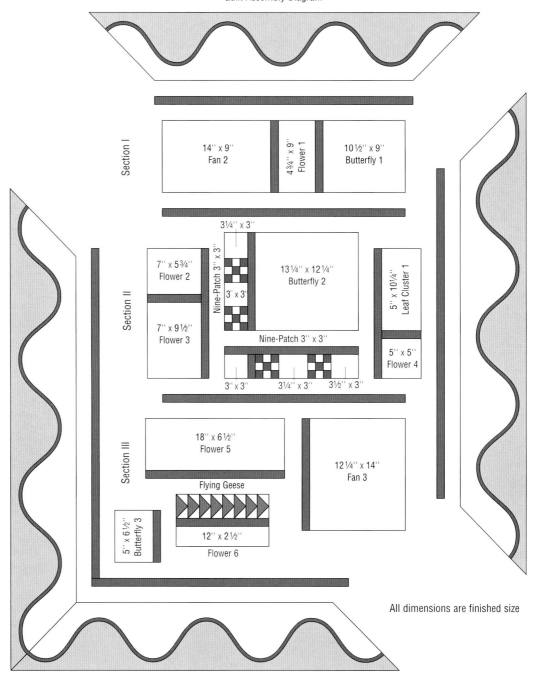

Section I

14" x 9"
Fan 2

4¾" x 9"
Flower 1

10½" x 9"
Butterfly 1

3¼" x 3"

Section II

7" x 5¾"
Flower 2

Nine-Patch 3" x 3"

13¼" x 12¼"
Butterfly 2

5" x 10¼"
Leaf Cluster 1

3" x 3"

7" x 9½"
Flower 3

Nine-Patch 3" x 3"

5" x 5"
Flower 4

3" x 3"   3¼" x 3"   3½" x 3"

Section III

18" x 6½"
Flower 5

12¼" x 14"
Fan 3

Flying Geese

5" x 6½"
Butterfly 3

12" x 2½"
Flower 6

All dimensions are finished size

Appliqué the Blocks

1. Referring to Illustration 1, the photograph, and the Pattern Insert, prepare freezer paper templates for Fans 2 and 3; Butterflies 1, 2, and 3; Flowers 1, 2, 3, 4, 5, and 6; and Leaf Clusters 1 and 2. Press the templates onto your chosen fabrics, and cut out the templates, adding seam allowances (see page 9).

2. Sew the blades of Fan 3 together, working from the center out. Turn under the seam allowances as indicated on the pattern. Baste. Arrange all the pieces of each appliqué design on its corresponding background fabric (see Illustration 1).

3. Appliqué the designs in place. Remove the basting threads.

4. Trim the background fabric from behind the designs, leaving a ¼" seam allowance. Remove the freezer paper templates. Press.

5. Embroider the designs with outline stitching (see Illustration 2) where indicated on the patterns.

Outline stitch

Illustration 2

Assemble the Pieced Blocks

1. Join 2 small light triangles to each large dark triangle (see Illustration 3). This will form a rectangular "goose." Press toward the darker fabric. Repeat to make a total of 8 of these units.

Flying Goose assembly

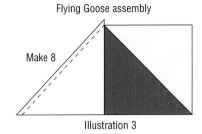

Make 8

Illustration 3

 Tip

Sew with the pointy end of the Goose on top, to make sure you don't accidentally nip off its point as you stitch.

2. Join the units together into one long strip of 8 geese. Press.

3. Referring to Illustration 4, sew the light and dark squares into rows of 3 squares each, alternating lights and darks. Make 8 rows of dark-light-dark squares, and 4 rows of light-dark-light squares. Press toward the darker fabric.

4. Sew the rows together to make 4 Nine-Patch blocks. Press.

Nine-Patch assembly

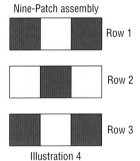

Row 1

Row 2

Row 3

Illustration 4

Assemble Section I

1. Sew the 9½" sashing strips to each side of Flower 1. Press all seams toward the sashing strips.

2. Sew Fan 2 to the left side of Flower 1.

3. Sew Butterfly 1 to the right side of Flower 1.

 Tip

Match the seamlines from row to row to get perfect intersections.

Assemble Section II

1. Referring to Illustration 1 and the photograph on page 20, sew a Leaf Cluster 2 to each Nine-Patch block. (Note that the leaf block backgrounds are not all the same size; refer to Illustration 1 for correct placement.) Sew these units into pairs. Press all seams toward the Leaf Clusters.

2. Sew the 3½" sashing strip to the remaining Leaf Cluster. Sew this unit to the side of the Step 1 pair that will be positioned horizontally. Press toward the sashing strip.

3. Sew the 12¾" sashing strip to the side of the remaining Step 1 pair. Press the seam toward the sashing strip.

4. Sew the Step 3 unit to the left side of Butterfly 2. Sew the Step 2 unit to the bottom of this assembled unit.

5. Sew the 7½" sashing strip between Flower 2 and Flower 3. Sew a 16¾" sashing strip to the right side of this unit. Sew this unit to the left side of the Butterfly unit.

6. Sew the 5½" sashing strip between Leaf Cluster 1 and Flower 4. Sew a 16¾" sashing strip to the left side of this unit. Sew this unit to the right side of the Butterfly unit.

7. Sew the 31¾" sashing strips to the top and bottom of Section II.

 Tip

Instead of cutting the individual sashing strips, you can cut long lengths of the sashing fabric, then cut these to fit as needed. Start with at least 380 inches of 1½" strips.

Assemble Section III

1. Sew the 14½" sashing strip to the left side of Fan 3. Sew the 18½" sashing strip to the bottom of Flower 5. Sew the 12½" sashing strip between the Flying Geese unit and Flower 6. Sew the 7" sashing strip to the right side of Butterfly 3.

2. Sew Butterfly 3 to the left side of the Flying Geese unit.

3. Sew the Butterfly unit to the bottom of Flower 5.

4. Sew Fan 3 to the right side of the Butterfly unit.

5. Sew Section I to the top of Section II, and Section III to the bottom of Section II.

Add the Borders

1. Sew the 2 longer inner border strips to the sides of the quilt top. Trim to fit. Add the remaining 2 strips to the top and bottom. Trim. Press all seams toward the borders.

2. Center and sew the 4 middle border strips to the quilt top, stopping ¼" from the corners. (These borders will extend approximately 8" beyond each corner.)

3. Miter the 4 border corners, sewing with a diagonal seam. Trim the seam allowances.

4. Referring to the photograph, draw a curved edge for this border (see Illustration 5). Trim off the outer edge of the border.

🐚 **Tip**

The border shown is symmetrical—you need to draw only ¼ of the border, then its mirror image; repeat these sections for the border.

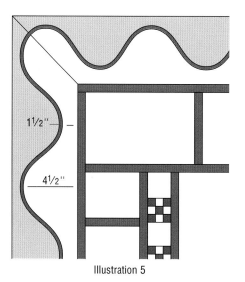

1½"

4½"

Illustration 5

5. Place 1 outer border strip right side up on a flat surface. Overlap it with 1 curved middle border (also right side up), centering the curved border on top of the outer border and overlapping the 2 pieces. The total width of the 2 border sections should be 8½". The outer border ends should extend beyond the inner border ends by approximately 3½".

6. Pin, then baste the two borders together, stitching through both thicknesses along the curved edge. Start and stop the basting 3" from each end.

7. Repeat until all 4 outer border strips have been added.

8. Miter the 4 corners as you did for the middle border, sewing with a diagonal seam.

9. Once the mitering is completed, baste the corner curves.

Add the Border Bias

1. Sew the strips of border bias together into one long strip. Press the seams open. Turn under and baste ¼" along both long sides. Pin, then baste this bias strip to the border, overlapping the cut curved line.

2. Appliqué the border bias to the quilt top (see Illustration 6). When you come back to the starting point, trim the ends ¼" longer than where they meet. Hand stitch the 2 ends together and complete the circle. Remove the basting threads.

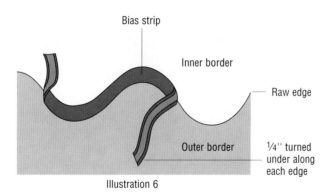

Illustration 6

Finish the Quilt

1. Layer the backing, batting, and quilt top. Baste.

2. Quilt as desired, through all the layers.

3. Trim the batting and backing even with the quilt top, squaring up as needed.

4. Bind, making double-fold binding with the cut strip.

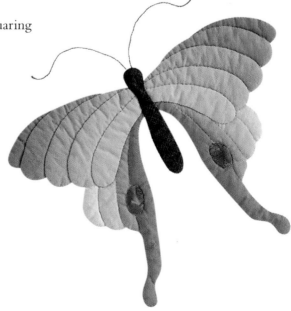

Peacock Fans

Finished size
32'' x 32''

Difficulty level

These peacock-blue fans display your prettiest print fabrics in all their glory. And they must be Irish, too—the decorative Celtic work in the corners of the borders reveals their ancestry. This setting would make a fun sampler quilt—pick four fans or other motifs from the Pattern Insert and make them from coordinating fabrics.

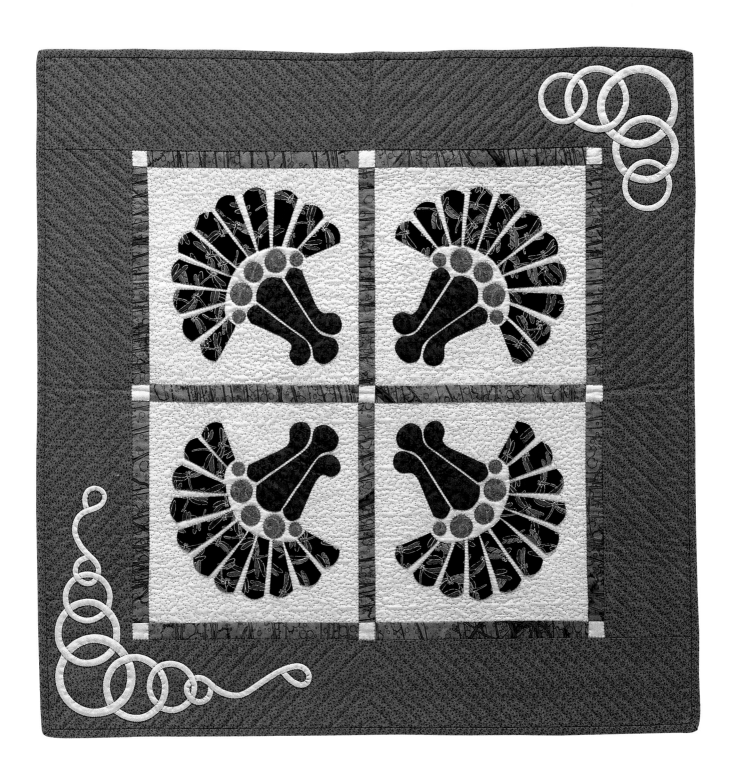

Materials and Cutting

FABRICS AND SUPPLIES	YARDAGE	PIECES NEEDED	NUMBER	CUT SIZE	FINISHED SIZE
Light	1 yard	Background squares	4	10½'' x 10½''	10" x 10"
		Sashing squares	9	1½'' x 1½''	1" x 1"
		Celtic strips*		1⅛'' x 171''	
Medium	Fat quarter	Sashing strips	12	1½'' x 10½''	1" x 10"
Dark	1 yard	Border	2	5" x 23½''	4½" x 23"
			2	5" x 32½''	4½" x 32"
		Binding		2¼" x 142''	
Dark	Fat quarter	Fan blades	44	See pattern	
Medium-dark	⅛ yard	Fan circles	20	See pattern	
Medium	⅛ yard	Fat quarter	12	See pattern	
Batting				36" x 36"	
Backing	1⅛ yards			36" x 36"	

*Cut on the bias.

Directions

Appliqué the Fans

1. Use Fan 4 from the Pattern Insert. Prepare freezer paper templates for the blades, circles, and bases. Press the templates to your chosen fabrics, and cut out the templates, adding the required seam allowances (see page 9).

2. Turn under the seam allowances, as indicated on the pattern. Baste. Arrange the pieces on point (diagonally) on the background squares.

3. Appliqué the fan in place. Remove the basting threads.

4. Trim the background fabric from behind the fans, leaving a ¼" seam allowance. Remove the freezer paper templates. Repeat for all 4 fan blocks.

Assemble the Quilt Top

1. Make 2 rows of blocks and sashing strips: Join 2 background blocks with a sashing strip, and sew 2 more sashing strips to the sides of the blocks (see Illustration 1). Press the seams toward the sashing strips.

Tip

You can reuse your freezer paper templates: Make the 4 blocks one at a time, carefully removing and saving the labeled templates for the next fan.

Tip

Make sure the fans are tipping away from each other when you sew the blocks into rows.

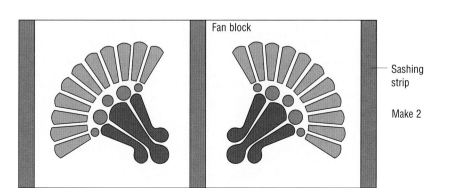

Fan block

Sashing strip

Make 2

Illustration 1

2. Make 3 long sashing strips: Join two sashing strips with a sashing square, and sew 2 more squares to the ends of the sashing strips (see Illustration 2). Press the seams toward the sashing squares.

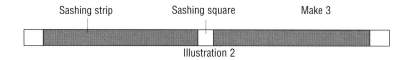

Sashing strip   Sashing square   Make 3

Illustration 2

3. Refer to the quilt photograph to join the block sections and the sashing strips together in alternating rows. Press.

4. Add the 2 shorter border strips to the sides of the quilt top. Press the seams toward the borders.

5. Add the 2 longer border strips to the top and bottom of the quilt top. Press the seams toward the borders.

Appliqué the Celtic Circles

1. Prepare the Celtic strips, as described on page 10. You will need two different finished widths of strips: 98" of $\frac{3}{8}$" width, and 73" of $\frac{1}{4}$" width.

2. For the top right-hand corner: With a compass, draw 3 circle-placement templates onto freezer paper: large ($3\frac{3}{8}$" in diameter), medium ($2\frac{5}{8}$"), and small ($2\frac{1}{4}$"). Cut out the circles.

3. Start with the largest circle template (Circle 1), and center it in the upper right-hand corner of the border, $1\frac{3}{4}$" from the outside corner (see Illustration 3). Press into place.

4. Pin the $\frac{3}{8}$" strip around it, leaving the starting and ending tails 1" longer than needed. Remove and save the template.

5. Iron the medium circle template in place for Circle 2, referring to Illustration 3. Pin the $\frac{3}{8}$" strip around Circle 2 as you did for the Circle 1. Remove the template. Adjust both circles so that the ends of the strips are hidden under each other (see Illustration 3), and trim the excess strip.

6. Add Circle 3 as you did Circle 2, on the other side of Circle 1. Pin in place.

7. Repeat with the small circle template, pinning the $\frac{1}{4}$" strip for Circles 4 and 5 in place. Make sure all the ends are trimmed and tucked underneath the other circles.

8. Appliqué all the circles to the border; press.

9. For the bottom left-hand corner: Repeat Steps 3 through 8. Prepare two additional $\frac{1}{4}$" Celtic strips, 12" and 14" long.

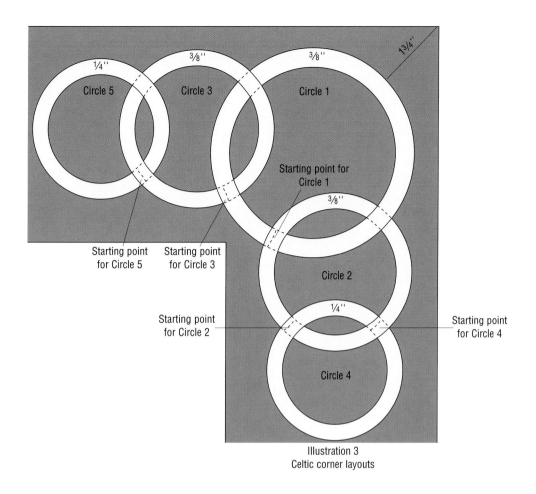

Illustration 3
Celtic corner layouts

10. Use ¼" strips to arrange the side designs freehand, referring to the photo and using the over/under rule.

11. Tuck the ends of the circles and side designs underneath each other, and trim the ends. Appliqué to the border; press.

Finishing the Quilt

1. Layer the backing, batting, and quilt top. Baste.

2. Quilt as desired, through all the layers.

3. Trim the batting and backing even with the quilt top, squaring up as needed.

4. Bind, making double-fold binding with the cut strip.

🌸 Tip

You can omit the Celtic circles for a simpler design.

Stained-Glass Fan

This fan's circular background makes it look more like a matted and framed work of art than a fabric quilt. The very dark accents in this quilt—the bias strips and borders—add drama and hold the attention of passers-by, just as a stained-glass window catches your eye as you walk by.

Materials and Cutting

FABRICS AND SUPPLIES	YARDAGE	PIECES NEEDED	NUMBER	CUT SIZE	FINISHED SIZE
Light	⅔ yard	Fan background	1	16½" circle	16" circle
		Middle border	2	1" x 22½"	½" x 22"
			2	1" x 23½"	½" x 23"
Medium	⅔ yard	Background	1	20½" x 20½"	20" x 20"
		Fan inserts	6	1½" x 4"	
			1	1½" x 2¼"	
Medium-dark	Fat quarter	Fan	1	See pattern	
Dark	1½ yards	Inner border	2	1½" x 20½"	1" x 20"
			2	1½" x 22½"	1" x 22"
		Outer border	2	3" x 23½"	2½" x 23"
			2	3" x 28½"	2½" x 28"
		Binding		2¼" x 127"	
		Bias for circle		1¼" x 56"	
		Bias for fan		1" x 100"	½" wide
Batting				32" x 32"	
Backing	1 yard			32" x 32"	

Directions

Construct the Quilt Top

1. Draw a 16½" circle template onto freezer paper.

2. Cut out the template and iron its shiny side to the wrong side of the fan background fabric.

3. Cut out the circle, following the edge of the template. (Because the edge will be covered by the bias strip, no seam allowances are needed.) Remove the freezer paper.

4. Fold the bias strip for the circle in half, wrong sides together, and press.

5. Align the raw edges of the bias strip with the edge of the circle, right sides together, and pin in place around the edge of the circle. Leave a tail at the beginning and the end of the bias strip. Sew the strip to the circle, using a ¼" seam allowance, leaving the tails loose (see Illustration 1).

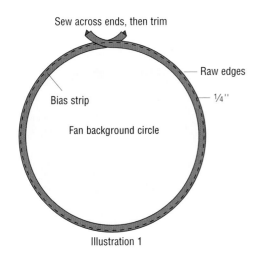

Illustration 1

6. Bend the tails beyond the edge of the circle, and sew across both ends, as shown. Trim the tails.

7. Flip the bias strip out (away from the circle) and press.

8. Center the circle on the background square, and appliqué it in place. Trim the fabric from behind the circle, leaving a ¼" seam allowance.

Appliqué the Fan

1. Use Fan 5 from the Pattern Insert. Prepare freezer paper templates for the upper and lower fan sections. Cut out and discard the areas on the pattern that are marked as inserts. Press the templates to your chosen fabrics and cut out the templates; do not add seam allowances, because the raw edges will be covered by bias strips.

2. Center the fan in the circle, aligning it so the fan points straight toward (perpendicular to) one edge of the background square. Baste.

3. Starting between the two fan sections, pin the fan bias strip so that it straddles the raw edge of the upper fan and the background. Continue around the fan, pinning the strip in place and looping it around the insert areas. When you get back to the starting point, continue around the lower fan, looping around the insert area.

 Tip Use the freezer paper pattern to help you place the loops of the bias strips, and refer to the photo for looping direction.

4. When you come back to the starting point again, trim the strip, leaving an end to tuck under.

5. Appliqué the bias strip to the background. Baste the bias strip to the edge of the fan.

6. Trim the background fabric from behind the fan, leaving a ¼" seam allowance.

7. Referring to the Pattern Insert, make freezer paper templates for the fan insert and the handle insert. Use these as patterns to cut insert pieces from fabric, and pin them in place behind the fan.

8. Appliqué the bias strip to the inserts. Trim any excess fabric from behind. Remove the basting.

Add the Borders

1. Add the inner border, sewing the shorter narrow dark strips to the sides of the quilt top. Press toward the border. Add the longer strips to the top and bottom of the quilt top. Press toward the border.

2. Add the light middle border and then the outer border as you did the inner border.

Finishing the Quilt

1. Layer and baste the backing, batting, and quilt top.

2. Quilt as desired, through all the layers.

3. Trim the batting and backing even with the quilt top, squaring up as needed.

4. Bind, making double-fold binding with the cut strip.

Rhapsody in Blue

It's been said that blue is the favorite color of many quilters—and this quilt certainly echoes that feeling. You can almost hear the music playing in the background as the bordered on-point fans dance across the top with the diminutive Nine-Patch blocks. The large spaces in the triangular background and the wide sashing strips offer plenty of opportunity for displaying your quilting talents.

Finished size
62½'' x 62½''

Difficulty level

Materials and Cutting

FABRICS AND SUPPLIES	YARDAGE	PIECES NEEDED	NUMBER	CUT SIZE	FINISHED SIZE
Dark	1⅔ yards	Block backgrounds	4	12½" x 12½"	12" x 12"
		Nine-Patch blocks	36	1½" x 1½"	1" x 1"
		Inner border	2	1½" x 54"	1" x 52½"
			2	1½" x 56"	1" x 54½"
		Binding		2¼" x 271"	
Medium	1⅞ yards	Nine-Patch blocks	45	1½" x 1½"	1" x 1"
		Block borders	8	1½" x 12½"	1" x 12"
			8	1½" x 14½"	1" x 14"
		Outer border	2	4½" x 56"	4" x 54½"
			2	4½" x 64"	4" x 62½"
		Fan arms	8	See pattern	
		Fan bases	4	See pattern	
Light	1⅔ yards	Sashing	12	3½" x 14½"	3" x 14"
		Corner triangles*	2	28" x 28"	
Assorted scraps	½ yard total	Fan blades	36	See pattern	
Batting				66" x 66"	
Backing	3⅔ yards			66" x 66"	

*Cut each square in half diagonally to yield 2 triangles (4 triangles total).

Directions

Appliqué the Fans

1. Use Fan 6 from the Pattern Insert. Prepare freezer paper templates for the fan blades, base, and arms. Press the templates to your chosen fabrics and cut out the templates, adding the required seam allowances (see page 9).

2. Sew the fan blades together as indicated on the pattern, working from the center out.

3. Turn under the seam allowances as indicated on the pattern. Baste. Arrange all the fan pieces in the center of the fan background block, placing the fan on point (diagonally).

4. Appliqué the fan in place. Remove the basting threads.

5. Trim the background fabric from behind the fan, leaving a ¼" seam allowance. Remove the freezer paper templates. Press. Make a total of 4 fan blocks.

Make sure the fans
are tilting in the
same direction in
both rows.

Assemble the Quilt Top

1. Sew 4 block border strips to each fan block, using 2 shorter strips on the sides, and 2 longer strips on the top and bottom of the block.

2. Sew the blocks and sashing strips into 2 rows, joining 2 blocks with a sashing strip, then adding sashing strips to the outsides of the blocks (see Illustration 1). Make 2 rows. Press the seams toward the sashing strips.

Make 2

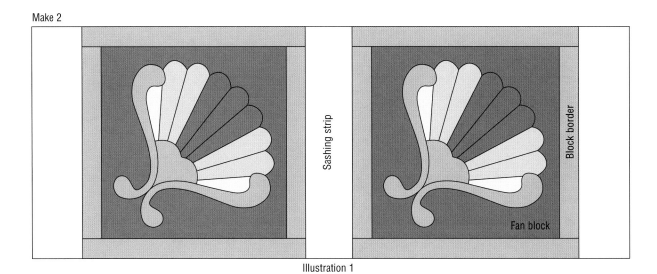

Illustration 1

3. Make the Nine-Patch blocks: Referring to Illustration 2, sew the light and dark squares into rows of 3 squares each, alternating lights and darks. Make 9 rows of dark-light-dark squares, and 18 rows of light-dark-light squares. Press the seams toward the dark squares.

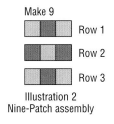

Illustration 2
Nine-Patch assembly

4. Sew the rows together as shown, to make 9 Nine-Patch blocks.

5. Alternate 2 sashing strips and 3 Nine-Patch blocks to form a long sashing strip (see Illustration 3). Make 3 long sashing strips. Press the seams toward the sashing strips.

Make 3

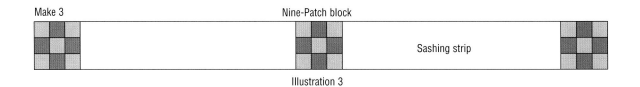

Illustration 3

6. Refer to the quilt photograph to assemble the quilt top. Join alternating long sashing strips and block strips; press. Make sure all the fans are pointing in the same direction.

7. Pin securely, then sew the 4 corner triangles to the quilt top. Press the seams toward the triangles. (The corner triangles are cut oversized, so there will be excess fabric on the edges.)

8. Square up the quilt top: Place the quilt top on a flat surface, and trim the excess corner triangle fabric. Remember to allow ¼" outside the Nine-Patch corners for the seam allowance (see Illustration 4).

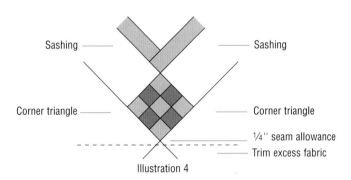

Illustration 4

 Tip

To stabilize a bias edge (like the ones on the long side of the corner triangles), iron a 1" strip of freezer paper onto the bias edge on the wrong side of the fabric. Sew through the freezer paper, then tear it along the perforations to remove it easily.

Add the Borders

1. Sew the shorter inner border strips to the sides of the quilt top; trim to fit. Press the seams toward the borders. Add the longer inner border strips to the top and bottom of the quilt top; trim and press.

2. Add the two shorter outer border strips to the sides of the quilt top; trim and press. Add the two longer outer border strips to the top and bottom of the quilt top; trim and press.

Finish the Quilt

1. Layer the backing, batting, and quilt top. Baste.

2. Quilt as desired, through all the layers.

3. Trim the batting and backing even with the quilt top, squaring up as needed.

4. Bind, making double-fold binding with the cut strip.

A Jewel of a Fan

Finished size
33½" x 33½"

Difficulty level

Bright jewel tones—the solid purple, pink, and red fabrics of the fan blades—make the fan seem to leap off the surface of this wallhanging. The eye-catching contrasting narrow borders and heart-shaped fan base combine to make a stunning quilt. Choose your wide border fabric carefully—you want something interesting but not too flashy, so it doesn't compete with the rest of the quilt.

Directions

Appliqué the Block

1. Use Fan 6 from the Pattern Insert. Prepare freezer paper templates for the blades, base, and arms. Press the templates to your chosen fabrics and cut out the templates, adding the required seam allowances (see page 9).

2. Sew the fan blades together as indicated on the pattern, working from the center out. Turn under the seam allowances as indicated on the pattern. Baste. Arrange all the fan pieces in the center of the background block, orienting the fan on point (diagonally) in the block.

3. Appliqué the fan in place. Remove the basting threads.

4. Trim the background fabric from behind the fan, leaving a ¼" seam allowance. Remove the freezer paper templates. Press.

Assemble the Quilt Top

1. Sew the shortest of the narrow borders to the sides of the background block. Press the seams toward the borders. Sew the next shortest of the narrow borders to the top and bottom of the block; press.

2. Sew the shortest of the wide borders to the sides of the block. Press toward the wide borders. Sew the next shortest of the wide borders to the top and bottom of the block; press.

3. Sew the shortest of the remaining narrow border strips to the sides of the block; press. Sew the next shortest strips to the top and bottom of the block; press.

4. Pin securely, then sew the corner triangles to the sides of the block. Trim the excess fabric so that ¼" remains outside the borders, as shown.

5. To complete the quilt top, add the remaining narrow and wide border strips as before, sewing the shorter strips to the sides, then the longer strips to the top and bottom, and pressing toward the borders as you add each pair.

Finish the Quilt

1. Layer the backing, batting, and quilt top. Baste.

2. Quilt as desired, through all the layers.

3. Trim the batting and backing even with the quilt top, squaring up as needed.

4. Bind, making double-fold binding with the cut strip.

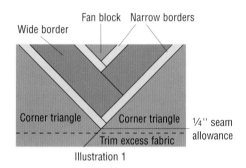

Illustration 1

Materials and Cutting

FABRICS AND SUPPLIES	YARDAGE	PIECES NEEDED	NUMBER	CUT SIZE	FINISHED SIZE
Dark	1¼ yards	Fan background	1	14½" x 14½"	14" x 14"
		Corner triangles*	2	14½" x 14½"	
		Binding		2¼" x 155"	
Bright	¼ yard	Narrow borders	2	¾" x 14½"	¼" x 14"
			2	¾" x 15"	¼" x 14½"
			2	¾" x 19"	¼" x 18½"
			2	¾" x 19½"	¼" x 19"
			2	¾" x 27½"	¼" x 27"
			2	¾" x 28"	¼" x 27½"
Dark	⅔ yard	Wide borders	2	2½" x 15"	2" x 14½"
			2	2½" x 19"	2" x 18½"
			2	3½" x 31½"	3" x 27½"
			2	3½" x 34"	3" x 33½"
		Fan arms	2	See pattern	
Assorted prints	Scraps	Fan blades	9	See pattern	
		Fan base	1	See pattern	
Batting				37" x 37"	
Backing	1⅛ yards			37" x 37"	

*Cut each square in half diagonally to yield 2 triangles (4 triangles total).

Raspberry Sherbet

Finished size
57'' x 65''

Difficulty level

This quilt is a mixture of an English flower garden and a frozen confection—the sherbet-colored fans seem to float above a cottage garden filled with daisies, camellias, and a riot of other blossoms. Be sure to take a look at the alternate version of this setting, which does not include the curved corners or the bias strip—you can assemble it in less time than it takes to plant the garden!

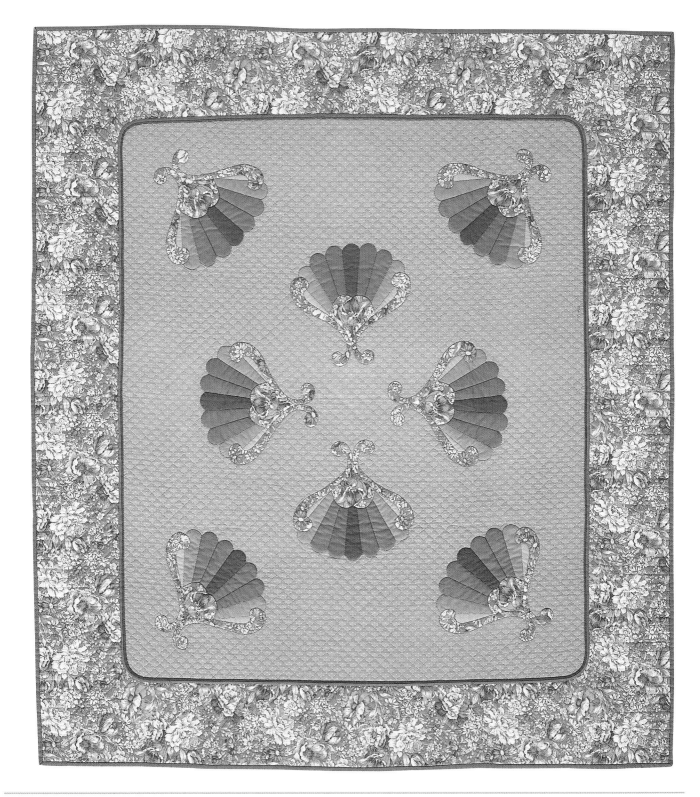

Materials and Cutting

FABRICS AND SUPPLIES	YARDAGE	PIECES NEEDED	NUMBER	CUT SIZE	FINISHED SIZE
Light	1½ yards	Background	1	40½" x 48½"	40" x 48"
Medium	3 yards	Border	2	10½" x 45½"	10" x 45"
			2	10½" x 57½"	10" x 57"
		Fan bases	8	See pattern	
		Fan arms	16	See pattern	
Medium-dark	1 yard	Fan blades	16	See pattern	
		Bias strip	1	¾" x 186"	
		Binding		2¼" x 259"	
Dark	½ yard	Fan blades	8	See pattern	
		Bias strip	1	¾" x 186"	
Medium	¼ yard	Fan blades	16	See pattern	
Medium-light	¼ yard	Fan blades	16	See pattern	
Light	¼ yard	Fan blades	16	See pattern	
Batting				61" x 69"	
Backing	3½ yards			61" x 69"	

Directions

Assemble the Quilt Top

1. Round the corners of the background: Use the Corner Template on the Pattern Insert to trace and trim the corners from the background rectangle.

2. With right sides together, sew the medium-dark and dark bias strips together along 1 lengthwise edge. Press.

3. Sew the bias strips to the background, keeping the dark strip next to the background. Ease the bias strips around the corner curves. Press.

4. Turn under ¼" along the raw edge of the bias strip. Baste. Set this center section aside.

5. Sew the medium border strips together into a frame, as shown in Illustration 1. Press.

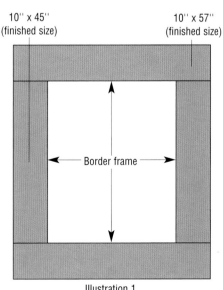

10" x 45"
(finished size)

10" x 57"
(finished size)

Border frame

Illustration 1

6. Place the border frame right side up on a flat surface; position the center section on top so the bias strips overlap the border frame by approximately 2" on all 4 sides (see Illustration 2).

7. Pin and baste the center section in place on the border frame. Appliqué the turned-under edge of the bias strip to the border. Trim the excess border fabric from the back. Press.

Appliqué the Fans

1. Use Fan 6 from the Pattern Insert. Prepare freezer paper templates for the blades, bases, and arms. Press the templates to your chosen fabrics, and cut out the templates, adding the required seam allowances (see page 9).

 Tip You will need a total of 8 fans for this quilt. If you remove the freezer paper templates carefully, you can use them to make more than one fan.

2. Sew the fan blades together as directed on the pattern, working from the center out. Turn under seam allowances, as indicated on the pattern. Baste. Arrange all the fans in place on the quilt top (see Illustration 3). The corner fans are 4" in from the border, the side fans are 7" in from the border, and the end fans are 11" in from the border.

 Tip Fold the background in half both ways and lightly crease; use these crease lines to accurately place the fans.

3. Appliqué the fans in place. Remove the basting threads.

4. Trim the excess background fabric from behind the fans, leaving a ¼" seam allowance. Remove the freezer paper templates. Press.

Finish the Quilt

1. Layer the backing, batting, and appliquéd quilt top. Baste.

2. Quilt as desired, through all the layers.

3. Trim the batting and backing even with the quilt top, squaring up as needed.

4. Bind, making double-fold binding with the cut strip.

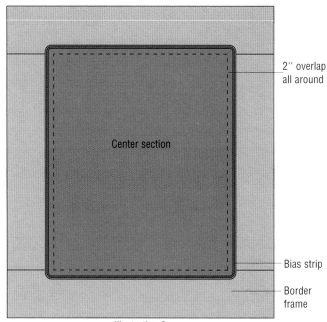

2" overlap all around

Center section

Bias strip

Border frame

Illustration 2

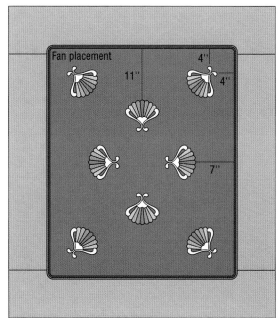

Fan placement

4"

11"

4"

7"

Illustration 3

Alternate Setting

If you prefer a simpler design, leave out the inner bias border and eliminate the curved corners of the center section. Follow the table below for yardage and cutting.

Directions

1. Appliqué the fans to the background (see page 40).

2. Sew the 2 longer inner border strips to the sides of the quilt top, pressing the seams toward the border strips.

3. Sew the 2 shorter inner border strips to the top and bottom of the quilt top; press toward the border.

4. Sew the 2 shorter outer border strips to the sides of the quilt top; press toward the border.

5. Sew the 2 longer outer border strips to the top and bottom of the quilt top; press toward the border.

6. Finish the quilt (see page 40).

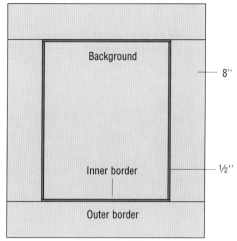

Alternate Layout

Materials and Cutting

FABRICS AND SUPPLIES	YARDAGE	PIECES NEEDED	NUMBER	CUT SIZE	FINISHED SIZE
Light	1½ yards	Background	1	40½" x 48½"	40" x 48"
Medium	2¼ yards	Outer border	2	8½" x 49½"	8" x 49"
			2	8½" x 57½"	8" x 57"
		Fan bases	8	See pattern	
		Fan arms	16	See pattern	
Dark	1½ yards*	Inner border	2	1" x 48½"	½" x 48"
			2	1" x 41½"	½" x 41"
		Fan blades	8	See pattern	
Medium	¼ yard	Fan blades	16	See pattern	
Medium-dark	⅔ yard	Fan blades	16	See pattern	
		Binding		2¼" x 259"	
Medium-light	¼ yard	Fan blades	16	See pattern	
Light	¼ yard	Fan blades	16	See pattern	
Batting				61" x 69"	
Backing	3½ yards			61" x 69"	

*For unpieced borders; if you piece your border strips, purchase ½ yard.

Greek Odyssey

The Mediterranean colors, formal fabric choices, and architecture-like shapes of the arms and bases of these fans give this quilt an exotic, foreign look. Enclosed by a double swag border and set off by quilted wreaths, each fan in this quilt makes its own statement. You'll have fun choosing fabrics—and fans!—for this quilt ... good luck limiting yourself to only seven!

Materials and Cutting

FABRICS AND SUPPLIES	YARDAGE	PIECES NEEDED	NUMBER	CUT SIZE	FINISHED SIZE
Very dark	¾ yard	Side outer scallops	16	See pattern	
		Corner outer scallops	4	See pattern	
Medium dark	⅔ yard	Side inner scallops	16	See pattern	
		Corner inner scallops	4	See pattern	
Dark	Scraps	Scallop circles	40	See pattern	
Light	5½ yards	Background	1	60½" x 88½"	60" x 88"
		Binding		2¼" x 310"	
Brights and mediums	Scraps and/or fat quarters	Fan pieces		See patterns	
Batting				64" x 92"	
Backing	5¼ yards			64" x 92"	

Directions

Appliqué the Border

1. Use the Border Scallops pattern on the Pattern Insert to prepare freezer paper templates for 16 side scallops and 4 corner scallops (make separate templates for the inner and outer pieces of each scallop). In the quilt in the photo, a very dark fabric was used for the outer scallops, and a medium–dark fabric was used for the inner scallops. Also make templates for 20 large circles and 20 small circles. Press the templates to your chosen fabrics, and cut out the templates, adding the required seam allowances (see page 9). Turn under the seam allowances, as indicated on the patterns. Baste.

 Tip The freezer paper templates can be reused; remove them carefully from one fabric, and you can re-press them onto another.

2. Arrange the scallops around the outer edge of the background rectangle (see Illustration 1 on page 44). Start with the center scallop on a long side of the rectangle, placing the outside tip of the scallop curve 4" from the raw edge of the background. Pin and baste in place.

 Tip Fold the background rectangle in half in both directions, and lightly crease the folds to use as placement guides for the scallops and fans.

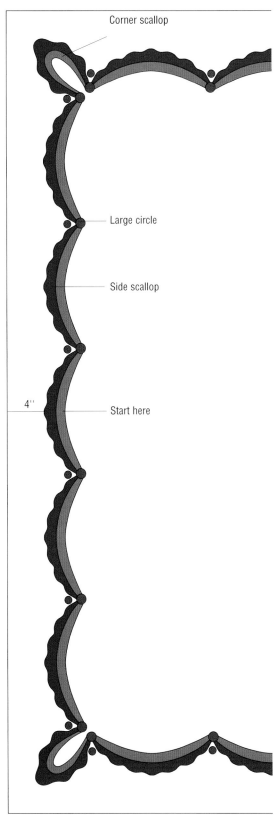

Corner scallop

Large circle

Side scallop

4"

Start here

Illustration 1
Scallop placement

3. Pin a scallop on each side of this first scallop, leaving just enough room for 1 large circle (about 1"), which will overlap the raw edges.

4. Add 2 more scallops, one on each end, completing the side. Repeat for the opposite side, then for the ends (which have only 3 scallops each).

5. Add the corner scallops, pinning the circles in place to make sure your placement is correct. Adjust as necessary, then appliqué the scallops in place.

6. Appliqué the large circles in place. Pin the small circles in place, ¼" from the large circles, toward the outside edge. Appliqué in place.

7. Remove all basting threads. Cut away the background fabric from behind the scallops and circles, leaving a ¼" seam allowance. Remove the freezer paper templates. Press.

Appliqué the Fans

1. There are 7 fans. Use Fans 1, 6, 7, 8, 9, 10, and 11 from the Pattern Insert. For Fan 1, do not include the rounded tops, but do include the circles that span the blades. Prepare a freezer paper template for each piece. Press the templates to your chosen fabrics, and cut out the templates, adding the required seam allowances (see page 9).

2. Sew the fan blades together as indicated on the patterns, working from the center out. Turn under the seam allowances, as indicated on the patterns. Baste. Arrange all the fans in place on the background fabric, inside the scalloped border (see Illustration 2). The outside edges of the fans should be at least 10" from the edge of the background fabric. Center the fans on the border scallops, referring to the photo.

3. Appliqué the fans in place. Remove the basting threads.

4. Trim the background fabric from behind the fans, leaving a ¼" seam allowance. Remove the freezer paper templates. Press.

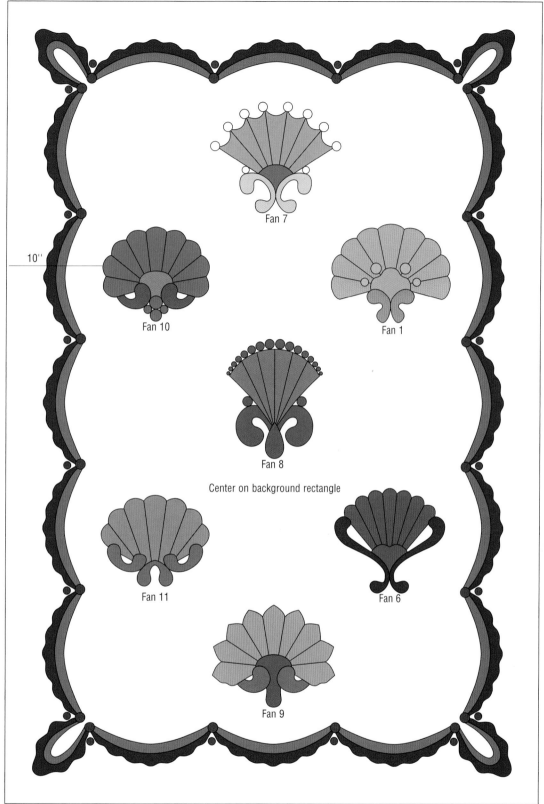

10''

Fan 7

Fan 10

Fan 1

Fan 8

Center on background rectangle

Fan 11

Fan 6

Fan 9

Illustration 2
Fan placement

Finish the Quilt

1. Layer the backing, batting, and appliquéd quilt top. Baste.

2. Quilt as desired, through all the layers.

3. Trim the batting and backing even with the quilt top, squaring up as needed.

4. Bind, making double-fold binding with the cut strip.

 Tip

For a simpler design, appliqué a grouping of fans onto a rectangle, then add straight borders, eliminating the scallops.

Scattered Marbles

This little quilt will give you plenty of practice appliquéing circles. It's almost like someone dropped a handful of marbles on top of the fan—which is also made of marbled fabric. This quilt has a *trompe-l'oeil* (fool-the-eye) effect: The light circles give the effect of cutouts that span the fan blades. The arches that interrupt the circular frame add just a little more interest.

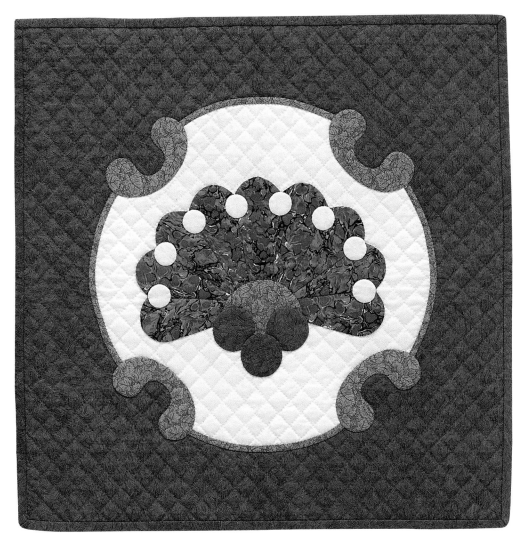

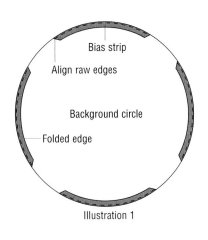

Illustration 1

Directions

Assemble the Center

1. Fold the 4 bias strips in half lengthwise, wrong sides together, and press.

2. Position the raw edges of the bias strips even with the raw edge of the background circle. Referring to Illustration 1, space the strips evenly, leaving room for the arches. Stitch the strips in place.

3. Flip the bias strips out and away from the circle; press.

4. Center this circle on the background square, right side up, and baste the circle in place.

Appliqué the Arches and Fan

1. Use the Arch Pattern on the Pattern Insert to make freezer paper templates for 4 arches. Press the shiny side of the templates to the wrong side of your fabric. Cut out the templates, adding the required seam allowances (see page 9).

2. Turn under the seam allowances around the edges of the arches, and position the arches so they cover the raw edges of the bias strips. Baste in place.

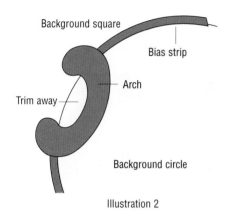

Illustration 2

3. Trim the circle fabric where it protrudes beyond the arches on the outside (see Illustration 2).

4. Appliqué the circle and arches in place. Remove the basting stitches.

5. Trim away the background fabric from behind the circle and the arches, leaving a ¼" seam allowance. Remove the freezer paper templates.

6. Using Fan 12 from the Pattern Insert, prepare freezer paper templates for the blades, base, circles, and arms. Press the templates to your chosen fabrics and cut out the templates, adding the required seam allowances (see page 9).

7. Sew the fan blades together as directed on the pattern, working from the center out. Turn under the seam allowances, as indicated on the pattern. Baste. Arrange all the pieces in the center of the background circle, aligning the center blade to point straight toward (perpendicular to) one background edge.

8. Appliqué the fan in place. Remove the basting threads.

9. Trim the excess background fabric from behind the fan, leaving a ¼" seam allowance. Remove the freezer paper templates. Press.

Finish the Quilt

1. Layer the backing, batting, and quilt top. Baste.

2. Quilt as desired, through all the layers.

3. Trim the batting and backing even with the quilt top, squaring up as needed.

4. Bind, making double-fold binding with the cut strip.

Materials and Cutting

FABRICS AND SUPPLIES	YARDAGE	PIECES NEEDED	NUMBER	CUT SIZE	FINISHED SIZE
Light	Fat quarter	Fan background	1	16½" circle	16" circle
		Fan circles	8	See pattern	
Medium	Fat quarter	Bias strips	4	1" x 9"	
		Fan base	1	See pattern	
		Arches	4	See pattern	
Dark	⅞ yard	Background	1	24½" x 24½"	24" x 24"
		Fan arm circles	3	See pattern	
		Binding		2¼" x 110"	
Dark print	Fat quarter	Fan blades	9	See pattern	
Batting				28" x 28"	
Backing	⅞ yard			28" x 28"	

Climbing Roses

The recipe for success when making this beauty of a quilt? Take one bold floral fabric, add two gradated borders, and finish off with a gently winding leafy vine. If that seems too overwhelming, simplify the setting and focus on the fans. Any pretty or playful print will work well in this "fussy-cut" fan—the theme and colors are limited only by your imagination.

Materials and Cutting

FABRICS AND SUPPLIES	YARDAGE	PIECES NEEDED	NUMBER	CUT SIZE	FINISHED SIZE
Very light	⅞ yard	Block backgrounds	5	12½" x 12½"	12" x 12"
Light	⅔ yard (for pieced borders)	Inner block border	12	1½" x 15"	1" x varies
		Inner quilt border	2	1¾" x 42"	1¼" x 40"
			2	1¾" x 44"	1¼" x 42½"
Medium	⅔ yard (for pieced borders)	Outer block border	12	1½" x 18"	1" x varies
		Middle quilt border	2	1¾" x 44"	1¼" x 42½"
			2	1¾" x 47"	1¼" x 45"
Medium-dark	1 yard	Side triangles*	1	18" x 18"	
		Corner triangles**	2	12½" x 12½"	
Dark	1½ yards	Outer quilt border	2	3½" x 47"	3" x 45"
			2	3½" x 53"	3" x 51"
		Binding		2¼" x 218"	
		Fan arms	10	See pattern	
Medium prints	⅔ yard total	Fan blades	45	See pattern	
		Fan bases	5	See pattern	
Assorted green scraps	⅓ yard total	Leaves	56	See patterns	
Medium green	1 yard	Bias strips (vine)		⅞" x 320"	¼" wide
Batting				55" x 55"	
Backing	3¼ yards			55" x 55"	

*Cut the square in half diagonally in both directions to yield 4 triangles.
**Cut each square in half diagonally to yield 2 triangles (4 triangles total).

Directions

Appliqué the Fans

1. Use Fan 10 from the Pattern Insert, and omit the lower 3 circles at the base. Prepare freezer paper templates for the blades, arms, and circles. Press the templates to your chosen fabrics and cut out the templates, adding the required seam allowances (see page 9). You will need a total of 5 fans.

2. Sew the fan blades together as indicated on the pattern, working from the center out. Turn under the seam allowances, as indicated on the pattern. Baste. Arrange each set of fan pieces on point (diagonally) in the center of a background square.

3. Appliqué the fans in place. Remove the basting threads.

4. Trim the background fabric from behind each fan, leaving a ¼" seam allowance. Remove the freezer paper templates. Press.

Piece the Quilt Top

1. Place a side triangle right side up on a flat surface, with the point facing you. Pin and sew an outer block border strip to the right-hand short side of the triangle, aligning the raw edges of the end of the strip and the point of the triangle that faces you (see Illustration 1). Press the seam toward the border strip. Leave the loose end untrimmed.

2. Sew a second outer block border strip to the left-hand short side of the triangle, aligning the raw edge of the end of the strip with the side of the previous block border strip. Press toward the border. Leave the end untrimmed.

3. In the same manner, add the inner block border strips, aligning the raw edges of the ends of the strips as before. Repeat for all 4 side triangles.

4. Place a corner triangle right side up on a flat surface, with the point facing you. Center, pin, and sew an outer block border strip to the long edge of the triangle. Press the seams toward the border strip, and leave the ends untrimmed (see Illustration 2).

5. Center, pin and sew an inner block border strip to the outer block border strip. Press toward the inner strip, and leave the ends untrimmed (see Illustration 2).

6. Referring to Illustration 3, center, pin, and sew side triangles to each side of 2 of the fan blocks.

7. Sew the remaining 3 fan blocks into a row.

8. Join the 3 rows together.

> **Tip** Refer to the photograph to orient the fan blocks correctly; when the quilt is assembled, all the fans should point in the same direction.

9. Add the 4 corner triangles, pivoting at the corners to create a mitered seam. Trim the ends of the block border strips; press.

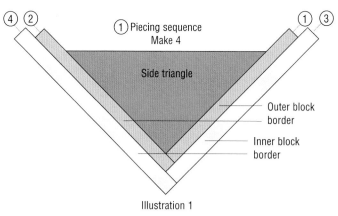

① Piecing sequence
Make 4

Side triangle

Outer block border

Inner block border

Illustration 1

> **Tip** Make sure you add the outer block border strip first, so that it will be toward the outside of the quilt when you assemble the top.

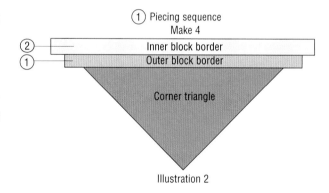

① Piecing sequence
Make 4

② Inner block border
① Outer block border

Corner triangle

Illustration 2

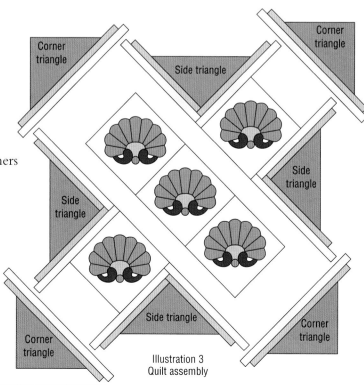

Corner triangle

Corner triangle

Side triangle

Side triangle

Side triangle

Side triangle

Corner triangle

Corner triangle

Illustration 3
Quilt assembly

10. Place the quilt top right side up on a flat surface, and trim the excess side and corner triangle fabric to square up the top. Remember to leave ¼" outside the mitered block border strips for the seam allowance (see Illustration 4).

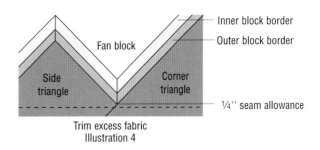

Trim excess fabric
Illustration 4

Add the Borders

1. Pin and sew the 2 shorter inner border strips to the sides of the quilt top. Press the seam allowances toward the border strip, and trim the strips even with the edges of the quilt top.

2. Pin and sew the 2 longer inner border strips to the top and bottom of the quilt top. Press the seam allowances toward the border strip, and trim the strips even with the edges of the quilt top.

3. Pin, sew, trim, and press the middle border as you did the inner border.

4. Pin, sew, trim, and press the outer border as you did the inner and middle borders.

Appliqué the Vines and Leaves

1. Using the Celtic Templates on the Pattern Insert, trace and cut 4 large and 4 small templates from freezer paper.

2. Iron the 4 large Celtic Templates onto the 4 side triangles, referring to the photograph and Illustration 5 for placement (about 2" in from the corner).

3. Iron the 4 small Celtic Templates onto the 4 corner triangles, referring to the photograph and Illustration 5 for placement (about 4½" in from the corner).

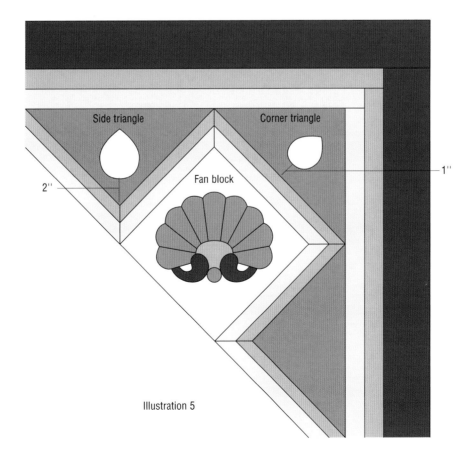

Illustration 5

4. Prepare the Celtic strip (see page 10). The finished strip should be ¼" wide.

5. Referring to Illustration 6, pin the raw end of the Celtic strip to the quilt top at a cross-over point on any one of the paper templates. (The dashed line in the illustration indicates the continuing path of the vine.)

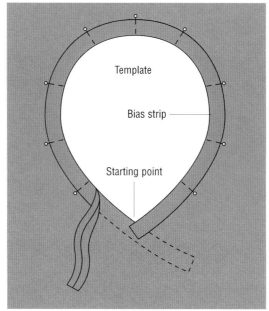

Template

Bias strip

Starting point

Illustration 6

6. Continue pinning the strip around the template, covering the beginning raw edge. Referring to the photograph, pin the strip in a gentle curve until you get to the next template.

7. Pin the strip around the next template as you did around the first one, beginning at the point of the template, and looping the strip over itself when you return to the point.

8. Continue pinning the strip around the entire border, until you reach your starting point.

9. Trim the bias strip and tuck the end underneath the loop at the starting point.

10. Appliqué the vine in place. Remove the paper templates.

11. Using the Celtic leaves patterns on the Pattern Insert, make freezer paper templates for the large, medium, and small leaves.

12. Cut out the leaves, adding a ¼" seam allowance, and randomly place the leaves along the vine, alternating the sizes and referring to the photograph for guidance.

13. Appliqué the leaves in place. Remove the basting threads.

14. Trim the background fabric from behind each leaf, leaving a ¼" seam allowance, and remove the paper templates. Press.

 Tip

If you pieced your quilt borders, hide the seams with appliquéd leaves.

Finish the Quilt

1. Layer the backing, batting, and appliquéd quilt top. Baste.

2. Quilt as desired, through all the layers.

3. Trim the batting and backing even with the quilt top, squaring up as needed.

4. Bind, making double-fold binding with the cut strip.

Alternate Setting

If you prefer a simpler design, eliminate the block border strips and the vine-and-leaf appliqué. Follow the table below for yardage and cutting. This quilt has a finished size of 40" x 40".

Directions

1. Appliqué the fans to the background blocks (see page 49).

2. Sew side triangles to each side of 2 of the fan blocks.

3. Sew the remaining 3 fan blocks into a row.

4. Join the 3 rows together, carefully matching the seams between the blocks. Add the corner triangles to complete the quilt top.

5. Square up the quilt top, trimming so that a ¼" seam allowance remains outside the points of the background blocks (see Illustration 4).

6. Sew the shorter border strips to the top and bottom of the quilt top. Trim to fit, and press toward the borders.

7. Sew the longer border strips to the sides of the quilt top. Trim and press.

8. Finish the quilt (see page 52).

Tip

Refer to the photograph to orient the fan blocks correctly, so they will all point in the same direction when the quilt is finished.

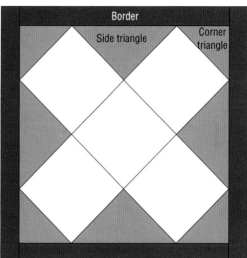

Alternate Layout

Materials and Cutting

FABRICS AND SUPPLIES	YARDAGE	PIECES NEEDED	NUMBER	CUT SIZE	FINISHED SIZE
Very light	⅞ yard	Block backgrounds	5	12½" x 12½"	12" x 12"
Medium-dark	⅔ yard	Side triangles*	1	18½" x 18½"	
		Corner triangles**	2	9½" x 9½"	
Dark	1 yard	Border strips	2	3½" x 36"	3" x 34"
			2	3½" x 42"	3" x 40"
		Binding		2¼" x 170"	
Batting				44" x 44"	
Backing	1½ yards			44" x 44"	

*Cut the square in half diagonally in both directions to yield 4 triangles.
**Cut each square in half diagonally to yield 2 triangles (4 triangles total).

Give It a Whirl

Finished size
55" x 55"

Difficulty level

This quilt is a perfect example of introducing a bit of whimsy to a traditionally formal pattern. The varying colors of the solid swirly, whirly fan arms and their matching sashing strips lighten the mood, and the coordinating Log-Cabin-like corner blocks echo the lightheartedness. If you like this quilt, try drawing your own different-shaped arms—wings, leaves, or a geometric shape might be just what you desire.

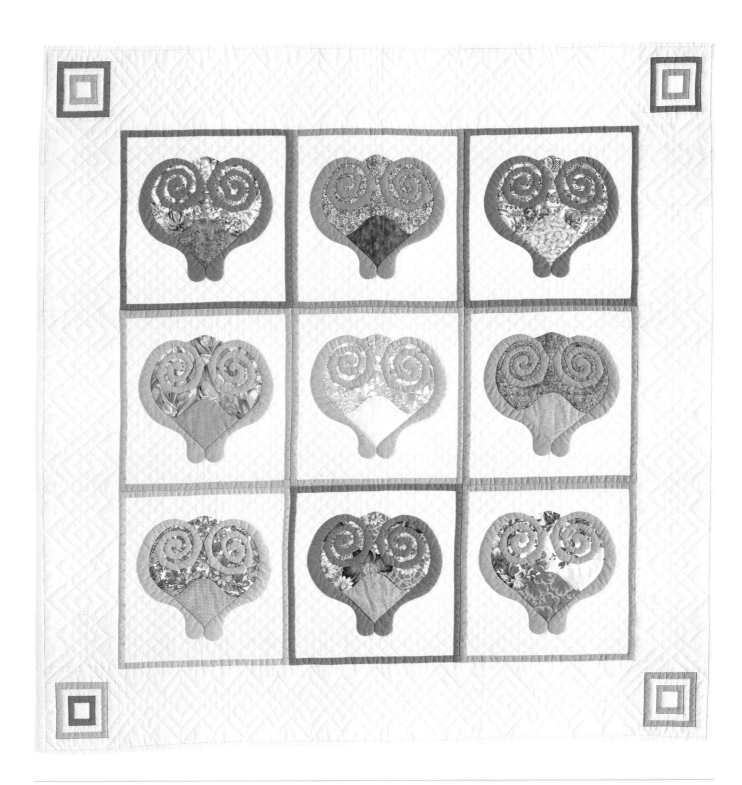

Materials and Cutting

FABRICS AND SUPPLIES	YARDAGE	PIECES NEEDED	NUMBER	CUT SIZE	FINISHED SIZE
Light	2¾ yards	Blocks	9	13½" x 13½"	13" x 13"
		Borders	4	7" x 42½"	6½" x 42"
		Corner block strips	4	1¾" x 1¾"	1¼" x 1¼"
			8	1" x 2¾"	½" x 2¼"
			8	1" x 3¾"	½" x 3¼"
			4	1½" x 4¾"	1" x 4¼"
			4	1¾" x 4¾"	1¼" x 4¼"
			4	1½" x 7"	1" x 6½"
			4	1¾" x 7"	1¼" x 6½"
		Binding		2¼" x 238"	
Assorted medium-light prints	8" x 10" pieces of nine different fabrics	Fans	9	See pattern	
Assorted light/ medium prints	5" x 6" scraps of nine different fabrics	Fan bases	9	See pattern	
Assorted medium solids	Fat quarter each of nine fabrics	Fan arms	9	See pattern	
		Sashing strips	18	1" x 13½"	½" x 13"
			18	1" x 14"	½" x 13½"
		Corner block strips	8	1" x 1¾"	½" x 1¼"
			8	1" x 2¾"	½" x 2¼"
			8	1" x 3¾"	½" x 3¼"
			8	1" x 4¾"	½" x 4¼"
Batting				59" x 59"	
Backing		3⅓ yards		59" x 59"	

Directions

Appliqué the Fans

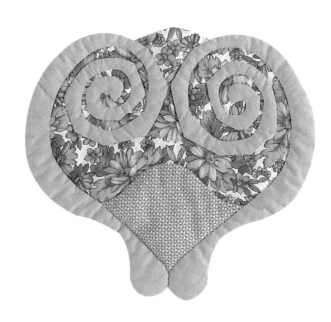

1. Use Fan 13 from the Pattern Insert. Prepare freezer paper templates for the fans, bases, and arms. Press the templates to your chosen fabrics and cut out the templates, adding the required seam allowances (see page 9). Note that you will cut a solid fan shape (shown on the Pattern Insert in gray) and pin the arms and base on top of it.

 Tip — To duplicate the quilt in the photo, cut matching arms and sashing strips from each fat quarter, and cut the corner block strips in pairs of matching colors.

2. Turn under the seam allowances, as indicated on the pattern. Baste.

3. Arrange a set of fan pieces in the center of a background square. Appliqué the fan in place. Remove the basting threads.

4. Trim the excess background fabric from behind the fan, leaving a ¼" seam allowance. Remove the freezer paper template. Press. Make a total of 9 fan blocks.

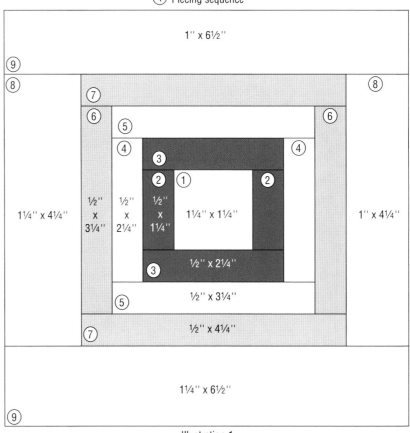

Corner square piecing sequence
Make 4
All dimensions finished size

Illustration 1

Tip

Two of the four outer light strips are ¼" wider than the rest of the strips. Make sure to add these wider strips on two adjacent sides of each corner block. These strips will be in the corners of the borders when the quilt top is assembled.

Tip

Match the sashing color to the fan arms.

Piece the Corner Blocks

The corner blocks in the border are made in a modified Log-Cabin fashion. Referring to Illustration 1, begin with a light square, and add corner block strips, alternating rounds of medium and light strips. Press all seams toward the outside of the block. Make 4 corner blocks.

Assemble the Quilt Top

1. Arrange your blocks in 3 rows of 3 blocks on a flat surface or design wall, as shown in Illustration 2. Referring to the numbering in the illustration, sew 2 shorter sashing strips to the sides of blocks 1, 3, 5, 7, and 9. Sew 2 shorter sashing strips to the top and bottom of blocks 2, 4, 6, and 8. Press the seams toward the sashing strips.

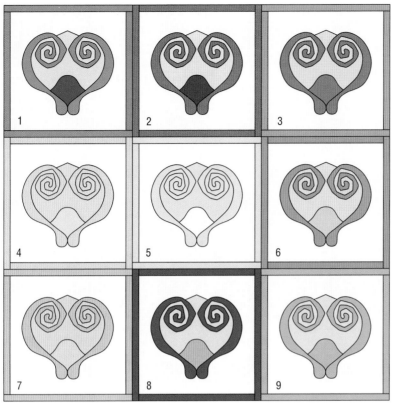

Illustration 2

2. Use the longer sashing strips to finish each block. Press toward the sashing strips.

3. Sew the blocks into rows, then join the rows together. Press all the seams in one direction. The sashing strips will appear to form a basket weave, cutting down on the bulk in the corners.

4. Sew 2 border strips to the sides of the quilt top. Press the seams toward the border.

5. Sew the 4 corner squares to the ends of the remaining 2 border strips. Make sure to position each corner square so that the 2 wider strips are in the corners of the border (see Illustration 3).

6. Sew these borders to the top and bottom of the quilt top. Press the seams toward the border.

Finish the Quilt

1. Layer the backing, batting, and quilt top. Baste.

2. Quilt as desired, through all the layers.

3. Trim the batting and backing even with the quilt top, squaring up as needed.

4. Bind, making double-fold binding with the cut strip.

 Tip For an easier-to-assemble setting, sew the fan blocks together in rows, separated by sashing strips. Sew the rows together, adding sashing strips between them, as well as around the outside. Add borders, and your quilt is complete!

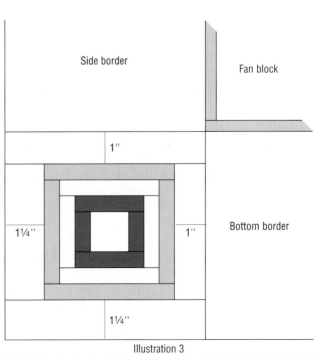

Illustration 3

Hands-on-Hips Wallhanging

Finished size
20'' x 20''

Difficulty level

This demure lady with her hands on her hips is surrounded by a cascade of appliquéd flowers. Her circular frame sits off-center on the background, giving her an air of mystery. (She would make a wonderful pillow for you favorite chair, too— see page 18 for pillow instructions.)

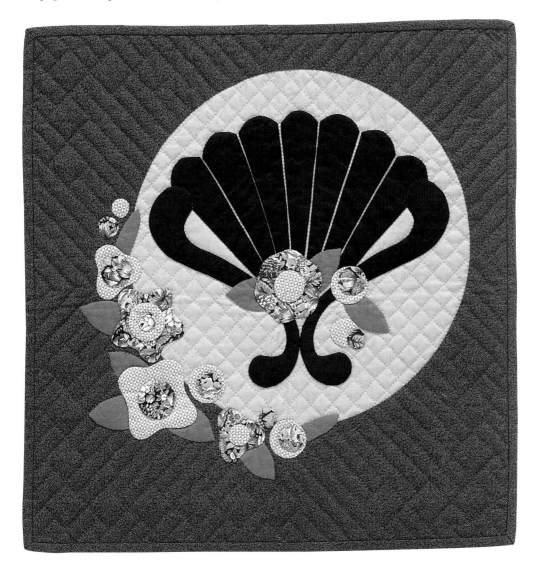

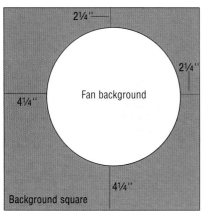

Illustration 1

Directions

Appliqué the Fan

1. With a compass, draw a 14½" circle template onto freezer paper.

2. Cut out the template, and place it shiny side down on the wrong side of the fan background fabric. Press in place.

3. Cut out the circle, following the edge of the template.

4. Remove the freezer paper and turn under a ¼" seam allowance around the edge of the circle. Press and baste the seam allowance in place.

5. Appliqué the circle off-center on the background square (see Illustration 1). Remove the basting threads. Trim the background fabric from behind the circle, leaving a ¼" seam allowance.

6. Use Fan 6 from the Pattern Insert. Prepare freezer paper templates for the fan blades and arms (omit the base and blade 4). Press the templates onto your chosen fabrics and cut out, adding the required seam allowance (see page 9).

7. Pick any of the flower, leaf, and circle patterns on the Pattern Insert to make freezer paper templates for the flowers and leaves. Press the templates to your chosen fabrics and cut out the templates, adding the required seam allowances (see page 9).

8. Turn under and baste the fan seam allowances, going completely around each fan blade and arm.

9. Arrange all the fan pieces in the center of the fan background circle, aligning the center blade to point straight toward (perpendicular to) one background edge. Pin the blades in place with just ⅛" separating them, then pin the arms in place, referring to the pattern and the photo.

10. Turn under and baste the seam allowances for the flowers and leaves, and appliqué the flowers and leaves in place. Refer to the photograph for flower and leaf placement. Remove all basting threads.

11. Trim the background fabric from behind the motifs, leaving a ¼" seam allowance. Remove the freezer paper templates. Press.

Finish the Quilt

1. Layer the backing, batting, and quilt top. Baste.

2. Quilt as desired, through all the layers.

3. Trim the batting and backing even with the quilt top, squaring up as needed.

4. Bind, making double-fold binding with the cut strip.

Materials and Cutting

FABRICS AND SUPPLIES	YARDAGE	PIECES NEEDED	NUMBER	CUT SIZE	FINISHED SIZE
Light	Fat quarter	Fan background	1	14½" circle	14" circle
Dark	Fat quarter	Fan blades	7	See pattern	
		Fan arms	2	See pattern	
Medium-dark	⅔ yard	Background	1	20½" x 20½"	20" x 20"
		Binding		2¼" x 95"	
Assorted medium scraps		Flowers, Leaves		See patterns	
Batting				24" x 24"	
Backing	¾ yard			24" x 24"	

A Gallery of Fan Quilts

Romance
This elegant pillow uses grayed colors and Celtic strips to great advantage. The upper edge of the fan gently waves for a look that's different from the traditional fan. The latticework isn't difficult—freezer tape and an acrylic ruler make short work of placing the strips accurately.

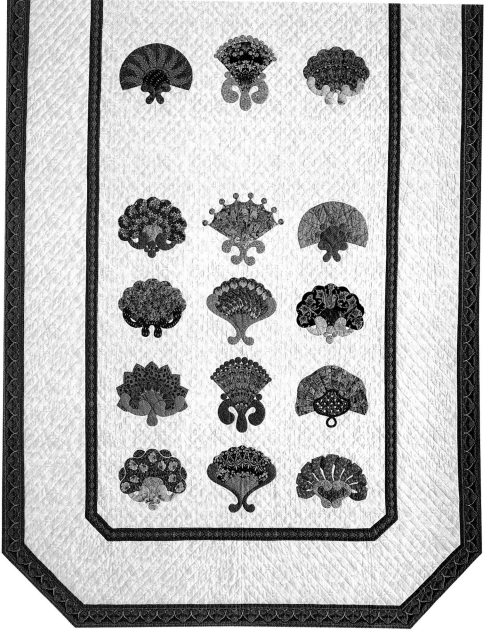

Trina's Delight
Once you start appliquéing fans, you might not be able to stop! Soon you'll be drafting your own designs, adding and modifying features to make each pattern uniquely yours. This bed quilt makes use of a pile of upscale gold prints that were waiting around for just the right use. Notice the "empty" row near the top: That's where the quilt gets tucked under the pillow.

Blue Rhythm

You'll find that a pillow is easy to put together from fabric you already have in your stash—and often the scrappy look makes the fan stand out against the background. Group the darker shades in the center of the fan, and the lighter colors toward the edges—or try the opposite, for a different look. A lacy border adds a fancy touch.

Blondie

This feminine wallhanging is easier to make than it appears at first glance. The leaf shapes are separate, appliquéd on top of the larger light background at each point. The pinstripe in the green border gives the illusion of a complex, fancy picture frame that surrounds what appears to be matted artwork.

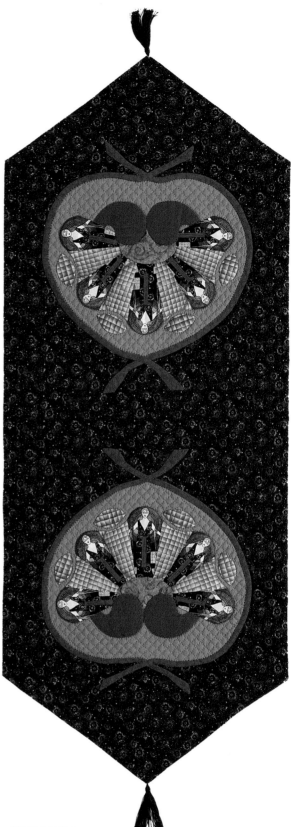

My Lady's Fan

If you have a stack of novelty print fabrics that you're just not sure how to use, try them out as fan blades. Very often there's a motif—like this stylish lady—within a fabric that's just right for a fan blade. Even if you don't think you could make a whole quilt out of your choice, sometimes a banner wallhanging or table runner can satisfy your need to use up the fabric or show off your fussy-cutting abilities.

Remember Me
The braided border on this little gem may look difficult, but it's just a series of short Celtic strips, pinned and sewn in place. The buttons and beads add sparkle and texture, but can be omitted if you like a simpler look. If you plan to hang an embellished quilt like this for display, be sure to use a sturdy batting, and quilt it closely to avoid sag.

Butterflies Are Free
The epitome of fussy-cutting: Each butterfly is cut out carefully, and placed just so, to fill the fan base. Look closely and you'll see that the fan blades are cut from the same butterfly fabric, but in a random fashion. The echo quilting in the background leads to some exciting secondary designs.

Cabbage Roses
This expanded version of the *Hands-on-Hips Wallhanging* (see page 58) takes advantage of *broderie perse*, a technique dating to late eighteenth-century France. In this technique, a motif is cut out of a fabric, then hand appliquéd intact onto a background, using a buttonhole stitch. The rose fabric in this quilt decorates both the fans and the bows.

Bride's Keepsake
This lacy departure from the norm is a wonderful way to display morsels of lace that have sentimental meaning. Even a damaged piece can make a beautiful keepsake reminder of the original. Gather up your bits and pieces, and arrange them on a pretty (but not distracting) background. Tack them down with tiny stitches, then quilt sparingly. Tone-on-tone prints or variegated solids work well for these creations.